*The Man Who Came Back*

# The Man Who Came Back

*Essays and Short Stories*

Neil M. Gunn

Edited by Margery Palmer McCulloch

Polygon

This selection © Polygon 1991
Introduction © Margery Palmer McCulloch 1991

Reprinted 1998

This edition published by Polygon
22 George Square
Edinburgh

Set in Linotron Sabon
by Koinonia, Bury and printed and bound
in Great Britain by Redwood Books


British Library Cataloguing in Publication Data

Gunn, Neil M. (1891–1973)
The Man Who Came Back
I. Title
823'.912

ISBN 0 7486 6114 X

The publisher acknowledges subsidy from the Scottish Arts
Council towards the publication of this volume.

# Contents

# Acknowledgements

I should like to thank Dairmid and Alasdair Gunn for copyright permission in relation to the essays and short stories printed here. My thanks are due also to the staff of the National Library of Scotland, Edinburgh and the Mitchell Library, Glasgow for their unfailing helpfulness and to the British Academy and Scottish Arts Council for small grants which contributed towards the research for the collection.

# Introduction

Neil M. Gunn (1891–1973) was one of the principal writers in the Scottish literary revival of the first half of this century, a revival which has come to be popularly known as the 'Scottish Renaissance' and associated in many people's minds with the Scots-language poetry of Hugh MacDiarmid (C. M. Grieve).

Gunn differed from MacDiarmid in a number of ways: he was a Highlander from Caithness in the north-east of Scotland; he was a novelist (and MacDiarmid had a small opinion of novelists generally, believing that poetry was the chosen art form); and perhaps most significant in the context of MacDiarmid's attempt to revitalise the Scots language for literary purposes, Gunn, like Edwin Muir, wrote in English, thus earning for himself Lewis Grassic Gibbon's epithet of 'a brilliant novelist from Scotshire'.[1]

Neil Gunn, however, was very much part of the early twentieth-century movement for Scottish literary and cultural renewal. Like MacDiarmid, and unlike those associated with the 'Celtic Twilight' movement at the turn of the century, he realised that a nation's literature and art could not be divorced from its social, economic and political life but that lasting cultural regeneration must go hand-in-hand with a regeneration of the nation as a whole. As his novels, short stories and many periodical articles show, he was not interested in antiquarianism, but wished to build a strong future out of a revitalised present. Yet, coming as he did from a Highland culture where the past was both valued for itself and perceived as having an essential relationship with the living present,

Gunn also worked for the rediscovering and nourishing of traditions and for an understanding of the past that would enable us to live meaningfully in our present and future.

In his 1958 study, *The Scottish Tradition In Literature*, the German scholar Kurt Wittig found that Gunn 'more clearly even than C. M. Grieve ... embodies the aims of the Scottish Renaissance',[2] and it may be that Gunn ultimately had a wider conception of what constituted 'renaissance' than had MacDiarmid. Both men saw it as an outward-looking activity which would take Scottish life and art back into the mainstream of European culture and both saw it as potentially bringing together the Celtic and Lowland Scots traditions. Yet MacDiarmid's insistence on the essential yoking of the non-Celtic literary renaissance to the Scots language in the end threatened to limit the potentiality of revival (as did his dismissive attitude towards fiction). Gunn's wider conception of culture and identity, on the other hand, held out the possibility of a more varied and far-reaching renewal.

Although Gunn accepts that for many nations a distinctive language is the hallmark of cultural identity, his understanding is that identity goes beyond language to shared cultural traditions and social patterns developed over long periods of time; to our relationship with our natural environment and to the complex of ideas about human life which has gradually evolved from the coming together of varied yet related living experiences. We can see this concept at work today in Scotland where there is a body of writing in all three of Scotland's languages arising out of distinctive linguistic, social and environmental experiences, yet which has a common cultural texture which can be identified as Scottish. The concept operates conversely in the contemporary international literary scene, where increasingly writers from Africa and Australia, Canada and the Caribbean, black and white America use English as their linguistic medium but produce confident and distinctive work which draws its strength from their individual diverse cultural roots. In the years since Edwin Muir's *Scott and Scotland* and the bitter language debate it provoked with MacDiarmid, it is Gunn's wider concept of tradition and cultural identity which has proved most fruitful in Scotland and internationally.

Gunn's literary career evolved not only in the context of the Scottish literary revival, but also in relation to the wider movement of modernism in Europe and America. And here it is less easy to place him. He was certainly aware of the innovations in literature and the arts in the early years of the century. In the article 'Scottish Renaissance', for example, published in the *Scottish Field* in 1962, he looks back to the twenties and the 'profound revolution [that] was taking place in literature ... One can remember reading the Parisian magazine *Transition* in the Highlands when James Joyce's *Work in Progress* was appearing in its pages ... But it wasn't even necessary to go abroad, for T. S. Eliot and Ezra Pound were publishing their poetry and criticism in London'.[3] He himself first came to prominence in that invigorating time, although his mature work as a novelist belongs to the 1930s and 1940s. Philosophically, Gunn's search for the 'atom of delight' in human life could be seen to run parallel to the loss of the 'radiant world'[4] lamented by Pound and many modernist writers, while his concern with myth and the traditional values of his Highland communities epitomised a search for the universal through the local that was characteristic of the period.

Stylistically, however, Gunn stands apart from the innovative techniques of modernism. His best prose is lucid and, like D. H. Lawrence, a writer whom he much admired, he has an exceptional ability to take his reader inside the sensuous response of his characters to the natural world or into the world of childhood experience. On the whole, one does not find in his novels the experimentation with language and form which is generally characteristic of modernist art. With the possible exception of *Highland River*, Gunn follows a well-tried traditional path in narrative form, while his predilection for an episodic structure may emanate from an oral story-telling inheritance. His city novels are thematically less notable for the urban experiences they portray than for the

traditional Highland values he offers as a counterbalance to
the sterility of the urban environment.

Gunn is in many respects closer to the nineteenth-century
Romantics than he is to the modernists. (And it is interesting
to notice that, perhaps because of their wish to make Scotland
anew, such an affinity with the Romantic movement is strong
in many Scottish Renaissance writers – even in MacDiarmid,
who in other ways is both modernist and postmodernist.)
Gunn's search for the 'atom of delight' is in actuality a quest
for an ideal which he believes is intrinsic to human life, not a
lament for a world gone irretrievably wrong. Similarly, his
advocacy of the traditions and values of his Highland communities is based in the belief that these traditions can revitalise
an urban world which has become dominated by materialism
and the demands of a machine culture and has in consequence
lost sight of its spiritual dimension. As with Wordsworth, the
experience of childhood and the contact with the natural
world are essential elements in his quest, although Gunn's
animism finds Nature more of an alien force than a foster
mother who teaches through love and fear. Yet for Gunn as
for Wordsworth the way into the 'other landscape', that 'sense
sublime/Of something far more deeply interfused' is very often
through Nature and comes about when one is least conscious
of the possibility. In his later life Gunn found a sympathetic
philosophy in Zen Buddhism in which he recognised an affinity with his own quest for the true way, with the traditions of
Celtic culture and with these moments of 'otherness', where
'self was a oneness with the infinite', which he found in the
Romantics and in Lawrence.[5]

As the foregoing discussion of his relationship with the
literary movements of the early twentieth century has proposed, the importance of tradition and its essential relationship with identity is a theme which lies at the heart of Neil
Gunn's work. It is a theme which animates novels of Highland
experience such as *Morning Tide, Highland River, The Silver
Darlings* and *Young Art and Old Hector*[6] and it is the impulse
behind the many articles he wrote for the *Scots Magazine* in
the 1930s, which complemented the Highland novels in their

exploration of the reasons for Highland decline and their attempts to point towards scenarios for regeneration. Gunn's investigation of tradition and identity in these essays took place in the political context of the 1930s and early 1940s when war between nations was both a dark memory and a new reality. He fully realised that 'nationalism' had become a discredited term for what many people considered to be a dangerous and discredited philosophy, and that to advocate it was to invite comparison with the forces which had led to the First World War and which were now again threatening Europe through the fascism of Hitler's Germany. For Gunn, however, true nationalism was not the jingoistic and perverted patriotism of the war-mongers, but an essential part of our cultural heritage, what he called in the essay 'Highland Games' 'a growing and blossoming from our own roots'. Nor was this concept of nationalism an inward-looking, parochial activity – the kind of thing Kenneth White has categorised as 'ruts not roots' [7] – but a rootedness which he saw as providing the essential conditions for a flowering into true internationalism.

One of Gunn's earliest statements of his conception of cultural identity is the article 'Nationalism and Internationalism', published in the *Scots Magazine* of June 1931. In this article he sees nationalism or patriotism as being 'founded in tradition, and we can no more get away from tradition than from ourselves. Indeed, immediately we get away from tradition, we do get away from ourselves'. For Gunn, a nation's traditions are the natural inspirations of its people ... 'And it is only when a man is moved by the traditions and music and poetry of his own land that he is in a position to comprehend those of any other land, for already he has the eyes of sympathy and the ears of understanding'.

In this definition of nationalism we see also Gunn's conception of internationalism and that insistence on the individual contribution which is prominent in all his work. He rejects ideological, theoretical moves towards a featureless internationalism, towards larger political groupings and increased centralisation, concepts which were in part a legacy of and a response to the national dissensions of the First World War. Such ideas seemed to him to be misguided attempts to solve the problems of international discord and economic poverty by the imposition of a standardised way of life. For Gunn 'the small nation has always been humanity's last bulwark for the individual against the machine, for personal expression against impersonal tyranny, for the quick freedom of the spirit against the flattening steam-roller of mass. It is concerned for the intangible things called its heritage, its beliefs and arts, its distinctive institutions, for everything, in fact, that expresses it. And expression finally implies spirit in an act of creation, which is to say, culture'. Internationalism, then, should not be seen as having the aim of 'a single centralisation of all power' or of 'standardisation' in our ways of life and beliefs – the 'neutral idea of the perfection of the beehive' which Young Art and Old Hector encountered in the Green Isle of the Great Deep in the novel of that title – but should be seen as a garden where 'each nation cultivates its own natural flower' and where 'the more varieties, the more surprise and pleasure for all'.[8]

Although developed in a very different international climate, Gunn's arguments appear equally pertinent today as the small nations of the former communist Eastern Block disentangle themselves from a faceless, centralised control and seek to rediscover their distinctive cultural roots, while the West moves somewhat uneasily towards greater European economic and political unity, simultaneously insisting on the preservation of individual national identity. His views remain relevant also to Scotland's continuing preoccupation with its fractured identity and to its see-sawing movements towards self-determination and self-responsibility.

The discursive essays reprinted in this collection all have this quest for genuine identity and rootedness at their centre. Apart from 'Nationalism and Internationalism', none has been previously collected and all are long out of print. Three essays, held in undated typescript form in the National Library of Scotland, are being published here for the first time. One of them – 'Is There a Living Scottish Tradition in Writing

Today?' – was broadcast on the Scottish Home Service in January 1959 as part of a 'Scottish Life and Letters' programme and would seem to have been inspired in part by the publication of Kurt Wittig's *The Scottish Tradition in Literature* in 1958. Internal evidence suggests an approximate date for the other two essays. 'For Christopher's Cap' is a tribute to Hugh MacDiarmid on the occasion of his receiving an honorary doctorate from Edinburgh University in July 1957, while 'The Myth of the Canny Scot', an ironic look at the role-playing of the Scots, can be placed by its reference to the contemporaneous launching of the *Queen Elizabeth* in 1938.

In relation to Gunn's exploration of rootedness, 'The Ferry of the Dead' and '"Gentlemen – the Tourist!": The New Highland Toast' explore the economic decline of the Highlands and the effect of this decline on the traditional way of life. While the latter essay argues against tourism as the panacea for Highland economic ills, 'The Ferry of the Dead' draws attention to the intensification of decline brought about by political centralisation and the imposition of economic criteria and measures inappropriate to local conditions. In Gunn's experience, one of the strongest adverse influences on the already weakened West Coast fishing industry was the government 'dole', a measure framed for industrial areas and unsuited to the conditions of life and work in the Highlands and Islands. In 'The Ferry of the Dead' as in the many articles he wrote about the Scottish fishing industry, he attacks an unemployment act designed with urban industrial conditions in mind but applied to an area such as the fishing coasts of northern Scotland where occupations are hazardous and catches and payments uncertain, where the working tradition has been one of a mixture of crofting and fishing and any other related activity which happened to come along. One cannot conform to the conditions of the dole under such a work pattern, and in order to conform to inappropriate conditions the old traditions and patterns of work are allowed to fall into decline. While Art in the fictional world of *Young Art and Old Hector* asked Hector to tell him the names of the old Clearance crofting areas, so that they would not become 'nameless' and thus die with Hector, 'The Ferry of the Dead' tells of an old seaman with a good boat who wants to pass on his seamanship and his knowledge of where the fishing banks lie before he dies but who can find no young men willing to go to sea with him. 'Why? Because the young fellows were on the dole or qualifying for the dole and would not lose the certainties thereof for the uncertainties of the sea. They would not even "give it a trial" lest their neighbours should "'tell on them".'[9] Once again Gunn's lesson of the thirties has relevance today, both to the continuing problems of the Highland economy and to the dilemmas faced by international relief workers in, for example, famine-stricken areas of Africa where the attempt to feed and keep alive starving populations by setting up relief camps works against the revitalisation of their abandoned natural habitats and the conservation and continuation of their cultural traditions. Gunn's 1930s attack on the debilitating effect of the dole on his Highland communities was not a complaint against giving money to the workshy, but a recognition – as we are seeing today in the international situation – that relief given with the intention of aiding a stricken community may, if the conditions of its administration go against the pattern of life of that community, in the end destroy rather than revitalise it.

In addition to its investigation of economic decline, 'The Ferry of the Dead' contrasts the contemporary Gaelic Mod with its ancient traditional counterpart and finds the contemporary activity lacking in vitality and purpose. 'At the core, it stands for the remembrance of things past and does not envisage a future in terms of that past.'[10] As 'Preserving the Scottish Tongue: A Legacy and How to Use It' insists on the choice of 'the living word on our lips' not 'the dead word in a dictionary',[11] so here Gunn cannot see a backward-looking Mod as a source of cultural life.

'Highland Games' is also preoccupied with the emasculation of traditions. In it Gunn appears to tilt humorously at the commercialisation of the Games with their travelling professional competitors who conceal embarrassing Highland dress under an 'obliterating overcoat', but his point is a serious one.

As he sees it, the essential tradition of the Games was one in which the competitors, like the Gaelic folk heroes of legend, were not men apart, but 'of the people, doing the day's tasks about steading or shore'.[12] This is the tradition depicted in *Young Art and Old Hector* where a boy like Art can aspire to be – and does become – one of these heroes. Through them he is enabled to grow and blossom from his own roots. Similarly in Gunn's novels of the sea and in the short story 'The Storm' included here, the heroes who sailed their fishing boats through the teeth of the storm to the safety of harbour and waiting relatives passed on their tradition of seamanship from generation to generation. In the essay 'Is There a Living Scottish Tradition in Writing Today?', Gunn remembers his astonishment when *Morning Tide* was criticised by a London critic for its avoidance of tragedy in its storm scene. For Gunn, 'to us, on the spot, the sheer wonder, the marvel, lay in the seamanship that so ordered the terrible fight in its final moments that death was given the slip with barely an inch to spare. Scenes like it were common enough all round our coasts – including the Islands, of course. That was what happened; that was the *tradition* in seamanship; and that was what I was paying tribute to'.[13]

While these discursive essays argue out the case for tradition, the descriptive pieces included here bring to life these traditions and the qualities of landscape and seascape in which they are rooted. Three of the essays – 'At the Peats', 'White Fishing on the Caithness Coast' and 'John o' Groat's' – were written in the early 1920s when Gunn was beginning to have some success as a short story writer, but before the publication of his first novel *The Grey Coast* in 1926. All three show the qualities of descriptive writing and social observation which were to distinguish his novels of life on the Caithness coast, the capacity to draw his reader into the landscape and life being described. 'The Dunbeath Coast', printed just before the publication of *Morning Tide*, is a paean of praise for that hard but heroic coast life, while the 1941 essay 'My Bit of Britain' returns in wartime to the theme of rootedness: 'When the blood fondly says "This is my land," it is at that moment profoundly in harmony and at peace. When it cannot say that, something has gone wrong, and it is that something that is the evil thing.'[14] This essay emphasises once again what Gunn saw as true nationalism or rootedness, as opposed to the synthetic patriotism which led to war between nations, and it includes these 'at peace' moments in the countryside referred to in 'Memories of the Months' (written also in 1941 under the pseudonym of Dane McNeil) where one can be alone with one's 'own soul' and where Gunn believed the roots of individual creativity and inspiration lie. The latest article to be included, the miniscule 'High Summer by a Mountain Lochan', printed in *Scotland's Magazine* in 1960, long after Gunn's novel-writing had ceased, captures in a few lines the very essence of that Highland landscape which had inspired him for so long.

In addition to these discursive and descriptive essays, I have included a number of short stories which have not previously been collected. Gunn husbanded his creative material carefully throughout his working life and several of the stories included here appear in a modified form in one or other of his novels. It seems to me, however, that such stories deserve recognition in their own right. Gunn's method in his novels was an episodic one, something which enabled him to incorporate previous short stories into his narrative structure without too much awkward seam-stitching. On the other hand, the original unity of theme in a short story and the impact and implications of its crisis can be lost when transferred to the wider, often polythemic context of the novel. This is especially true of a story such as 'The Dead Seaman' which later became one of many strands in the 1946 novel *The Key of the Chest* . 'The Dead Seaman' is a strong, tense story of human isolation in the midst of the pettiness and unthinking cruelty of small community life, its enigmatic tragedy played out in a cottage by the wild sea coast at a distance from the nearest village. There is a tragic inevitability and unity of action here which is dissipated in the context of the later book with its romance ending.

Another story which deserves recognition for itself is 'Snow in March' which was later modified to become a subject of reminiscence for the character Aunt Phemie in *The Shadow*. Once again the story has a life and import of its own which is weakened when it is absorbed into the detail of the novel. 'Snow in March' tells of a middle-aged spinster who takes a year's leave from her city teaching post to help her farmer brother after the death of their mother and is brought to the realisation of her own thwarted motherhood by the crying of the new-born lambs in a late spring snowstorm. There are Lawrentian undercurrents here, as in the novel of which it eventually became a part. Unlike the novel, however, the short story keeps such affinities subordinate to Gunn's own vision.

Two stories which have not been subsequently incorporated into a later novel are 'Birdsong at Evening', first published in the *Cornhill Magazine* in 1926, and 'Strath Ruins' from *Chambers's Journal* of 1927. 'Strath Ruins' is a story with a twist in its tale which anticipates the exhilaration of the hunt enacted in many poaching episodes in the novels which were to come. 'Birdsong at Evening' is an unusual contribution to Gunn's oeuvre. Written when he was in his mid-thirties and at the beginning of his writing career, it is a gently ironic tale of an elderly bachelor who finds new purpose and a new beginning in life in his retirement move from city to country. The *Cornhill* published copy, while essentially interesting, is marred by the over-writing which at times characterised Gunn's early short stories. The National Library of Scotland, however, holds a copy which has been significantly revised by Gunn and is much more taut. This is the copy text reprinted here and to my knowledge it has not been published elsewhere.

I believe that the short stories included are worthy of being brought back into print on their own account, despite the fact that some of them have had a second life as episodes in Gunn's novels. In addition to their intrinsic interest, their transformation gives the reader an insight into Gunn's working methods while they have their own contribution to make to his exploration of tradition and identity. 'The Storm' gives life to the tradition of seamanship referred to in 'Is There a Living

Scottish Tradition in Writing Today?', while 'The Man Who Came Back' of 1928 is another exploration of Gunn's recurring theme of the returning Highlander who can find no place in the physical homeland which emotionally holds his heart – a theme which he put forward in novel form in *The Lost Glen* (serialised in the *Scots Magazine* in 1928 and published in 1932) and *The Drinking Well* of 1946, and which appeared again as the play *Back Home* in 1932. 'The Boat', 'The Dead Seaman' and 'Strath Ruins' enact various scenes, both positive and negative, from the historical and contemporary life of these small Highland communities. All show the individual in relation to a rootedness in environment and traditions. And for Gunn in essay and short story alike, 'tradition is the environment in which the creative spirit is at home to itself'.[15]

*Margery McCulloch*
*Glasgow 1991.*

## Notes

1. Lewis Grassic Gibbon, 'Literary Lights', *Scottish Scene or The Intelligent Man's Guide to Albyn* (with Hugh MacDiarmid) (London: Hutchison, 1934), p. 200.
2. Kurt Wittig, *The Scottish Tradition in Literature* (Edinburgh: Oliver & Boyd, 1958), p. 339.
3. Neil M. Gunn, 'Scottish Renaissance', *Scottish Field* August 1962, p. 34; reprinted in *Landscape and Light: Essays by Neil M. Gunn*, ed. A. McCleery (Aberdeen: Aberdeen University Press, 1987), pp. 97-8.
4. See Neil M. Gunn, *The Atom of Delight* (London: Faber & Faber, 1956), passim; Ezra Pound, 'Cavalcanti', *Literary Essays of Ezra Pound*, ed. T. S. Eliot (London: Faber & Faber, 1954), p. 154.
5. See Neil M. Gunn, *The Other Landscape* (London: Faber & Faber, 1954), passim; William Wordsworth, 'Tintern Abbey', *The Poetical Works Of Wordsworth*, rev. ed. (London: Oxford University Press, 1936), p. 164; D. H. Lawrence, *The Rainbow* (London: Methuen, 1915), Penguin ed., p. 441, quoted by Gunn in 'Eight Times Up', *Landscape and Light*, p. 241.
6. A detailed discussion of all twenty of Gunn's novels can be found in the present writer's *The Novels of Neil M. Gunn: A Critical Study* (Edinburgh: Scottish Academic Press, 1987).
7. Neil M. Gunn, 'Highland Games', *Scots Magazine* XV No. 5,

September 1931, p. 414; Kenneth White, speaking at a conference held under the auspices of the Advisory Council for the Arts
in Scotland (AdCAS), Old Royal High School, Edinburgh,
2 June 1990.

8. Neil M. Gunn, 'Nationalism and Internationalism', *Scots Magazine* XV No. 3, June 1931, pp. 187-88.

9. Neil M. Gunn, 'The Ferry of the Dead', *Scots Magazine* XXVIII
No. 1, October 1937, pp. 16-17.

10. Ibid., p. 20.

11. Neil M. Gunn, 'Preserving the Scottish Tongue: A Legacy and
How to Use It', *Scots Magazine* XXIV No. 2, November 1935,
p. 111.

12. *Scots Magazine* XV, p. 414.

13. Neil M Gunn, 'Is There a Living Scottish Tradition in Writing
Today?', National Library of Scotland, dep. 209, box 9, No.83,
p. 1.

14. Neil M. Gunn, 'My Bit of Britain', *The Field,* 2 August 1941,
p. 136.

15. 'Is There a Living Scottish Tradition in Writing Today?', NLS
copy p. 4.

# *Essays*

# The Dunbeath Coast

## Caithness Your Home, 1930

The brown sails, the creak of the halyards to the heave-ho, our own skippers, the West Coast crews, and sunlight still on the bay as the boats stand out to sea. A natural sentiment may heighten the picture now, but I am sure that a quickening beset the picture then, for into the toil and the danger came the romance of the uncertain. Pausing in his game, or deserting his bait to the sellags, a small boy here and there would watch in a speechless quiet that brave procession, and vaguely in his mind would thrill the old gamble of the sea. The sea, swaying there in the bright days of the summer fishing, wheels of light flashing over it like bent girds, the swing and the rhythm, the hypnotic staring, and down below the water, clear and deep and drowning.

Then the young weathered face would lift again, and the eyes linger on the slow rock and dip of the boats in a small air of wind, feeling for the open, dip and rise. Who knew what they might not return with in the morning? Perhaps a few baskets, perhaps not a scale – but perhaps full to the gunnels. One of them might come in with a great shot, and all the others be light. No one could tell. And there *was* always one that his young eyes hoped for more than any other, not so much for the profit of it as for the pride.

And when the mind wandered in dream, was that not often the very time when the line jerked and a veritable cudding or even – for dreams came to life in those days – a red rock coddie

hooked himself and received the deadly heave? Excitement
enough there and pride, even if the mother of the house found
no more in it than evidence of dangerous rock fishing and the
need for admonishment. Nor did the prize always find a pot,
though it might secretly find a hake and glisten by the back
door in the dark with a ghostly fire.

But the morning – it was all waiting and watching and talk. In
the clean wooden gutting stations bare-footed games were
played from corner to corner, and shrill laughter echoed the
circling gulls. The boats were coming in. A long way off they
were known by their action and trim, and as each drew nearer
guesses were hazarded as to fortune. And the guesses came
remarkably near the truth. When she was 'pretty deep,' it was
time for the curers' men to get busy. The gutters donned their
oilskin aprons that rustled as they walked. Talk shot hither
and thither, and quick laughter followed many a sally. For the
life here was full and rich. In a remarkable way the community
was self-contained and self-sufficient, with its own games, its
own social life, its own vivid concern with the passions. True,
the finger of decay was already upon it; young men were going
abroad more and more; ambition to 'get on' in the great outer
world was casting its grey breath on this old homeland. But to
the boy of eight or nine that side of it was mostly hidden. Only
the thrilling life was seen of the men of the sea coming back in
the summer morning, handling their boats with expert skill,
swaying in their great sea-boots, quiet self-contained men
with quick eyes ready to light up in humour.

Down from the hills would straggle an odd man to get the
news. For the harbour was the life-centre to the croft-lands
behind. A good fishing meant prosperity all round. And
prosperity brought happiness and freedom from care. Youth
felt this by a gay intuition, and the scene would shift from the
harbour to the strath to wild Red Indian games, to river raids,
to long absences without food, absences that brought up the
maternal frown – with an effort.

It was a good life to have come out of. It is difficult indeed to conceive a better. For it was not all sunshine – if the sunshine has the trick of remaining. But even out of the bitter cold and the smashing seas of winter storms, there comes back, in the memory of youth, something heroic rather than desolate. We may now have all 'got on' to our hearts' content. We may look down upon the deserted fishing creeks of that iron coast and wonder what of thrilling life could ever have been in them. But some of us who would not swap our beginnings for the brick-and-mortar of kings, may also sometimes wonder with what qualities we could measure ourselves against these seamen who were our fathers.

# At the Peats

*Chambers's Journal, 1923*

Hardly a life but can be set athrill to some subtle loveliness or secret intimacy of the past by the sudden touching of one particular little note of the senses – a sound, a colour, an odour; and just as, amongst our senses we rely least on our sense of smell, so, with all the sweet justice of life's uses, do we keep for that particular sense the flower-like power of treasuring all that is hidden and rare and exotic. As with the individual, so with the race. And if there is any one thing that can bring the world of Gaeldom – Gaeldom present and receding into the dim, storied, heroic past – flooding the mind inexpressibly in a moment, it is the unexpected whiff of odour from a peat fire. Any still evening go up from the lowlands, the cities, the ends of the earth, to a Highland moor or glen. Peace you will find there 'come dropping slow,' and many other blessed things besides; but if the first whiff of peat-reek does not curl speechlessly round the roots of your being, does not send up a beating wave of feeling as inexpressible and old as the beginnings of things, then you are not of that glen nor of that moor.

I sometimes think that a very great work could be written on the fuels of the world, not from the calorific, industrial, economic point of view, but from this of the feelings they arouse in those who have been cradled by their warmth and grown to manhood through all the subtle, shaping, racial influences that are ever at play wherever a few gather round the mystic wonder of a fire – from the trappers and hunters of the frozen North round their aromatic wood fires, backed by the great white silence where instincts are keen and sure and death is swift, vast primeval austerity with the symbol of the wolf's fang, down to the acrid ammoniacal smoke and vapour given off by the dried dung cakes of camel and ox which make the common fuel of Egypt and India. 'Acrid ammoniacal' – are these the adjectives that would occur to a son of the desert returning from exile, when the first sniff of that same strange fuel greeted his nostrils? 'No one but God and me knows what is in my heart.'

So I suppose the book will never be written, because each portion would have to be created by a separate interpreter or poet, and each poet would be wholly intelligible only to his own tribe, for each would strike a particular sense note that would set surging the ageless racial feelings that are deeper than we know of.

Peat-cutting in the Scottish Highlands is not an industry; it is a family concern. Generally speaking, every crofter, cottar, or fisherman possesses his inalienable right to a portion of the peat-bank or peat-bog, a right descended from time immemorial. Here, near the Caithness-Sutherland border, every year towards the end of April he makes his arrangements for 'a day at the peats.' The winter has seen a fair inroad on his last year's store, and whatever else the coming year may provide, it must provide fuel. With fire, oatmeal, potatoes, and salt herrings, your true Highlander will still face much, though at one time, indeed, he could face everything.

So the first fine morning in late April or early May sees the little squad setting out for moor or hill with the distinctive implements of their craft and the necessary provisions in the way of bodily refreshment. It is to be a long, arduous day, and yet this annual event holds in it a half-pleasurable sense of excitation. The lonely moor, the remoteness from the grouped village or neighbourly crofts, weather possibilities, the sense as of picnicking curiously steadied and given a responsible twist by the underlying knowledge of necessity and fruitfulness (so dear to puritanic heart), and the picnic itself, with, if times are good, a little drop of the heather ale!

There is no impression of hurry. The 'bank' is surveyed with the keen eye of a quiet leisureliness. If a new bank is to be taken out, it is tested throughout its proposed length for depth of turf by digging and proving here and there. Many factors have to be considered, such as the quality of the peat, accessibility to the road, the 'lie' of the ground to assure proper drainage, nearness to neighbouring banks. When at last the course has been 'spanged out' from end to end, two parallel lines about four feet apart are unwound and run to its whole length, which, for 'a day's cutting,' will be, at least, a hundred yards. A day's cutting represents, roughly, about sixteen cartloads, each load being built high up, stack fashion, on the cart, and will last a cottage, normally using one fire, a whole year. It will thus be seen that, with all the philosophic reality of life in these remote places, a day's cutting is a day's cutting though the business last four hours or a week!

The gaffer gives the word, and the 'rutter' starts off along the line. The rutter is a two-handed spade, the blade heart-shaped and sharp. The immediate object is to prepare for the paring of the surface – that is, the removal of the uppermost six or more inches of heather-sod which covers every peat-bog, and which, of course, from a fuel standpoint, is useless. When this skin has been removed the black bed of the true peat is exposed. But the removal of this skin – the 'tirring' – is quite a strenuous business. Laboriously onwards moves the rutter, the full weight of the worker landing by foot and hands on blade-top and handle respectively, somewhat after the fashion of a gardener cutting a straight, deep line with a spade across a grassy lawn – only in place of the soft, yielding grass of the lawn are the tough, matted heather-roots of the ancient bog. Up and down and across, the work goes on till the whole area has been diced into sections not much greater than a square foot.

But while one or two workers keep the rutting in full swing, the rest are not idle. Immediately a sufficient area has been cut to permit of a start being made at tirring, the gaffer gets hold of the 'flauchter-spade.' This is also a two-handed spade, but altogether mightier than the other, in truth a tremendous weapon to be wielded by one man. About five feet long, it has a very stout and curved shaft. The blade is inserted under the first diced sod, and then, with the wide cross-bar of the handle gripped in both hands and touching body about the stomach, the brawny wielder 'puts his weight into it,' the concave curvature of the shaft assisting both in keeping the blade running at an even depth from the surface and as a lever every now and again to jerk the sods upwards. As the sods or 'faels' are thus having the ground very literally cut from under them, they are plucked from the flaughter-spade by a worker whose task it is to tidy them away in the best interests of the bank itself, always bearing in mind that horses and carts have to come in over the ground to take the peats at a later date in small loads out to the firm moorland road, and, what is very important, that the bank must not be left as a water trap for sheep and 'cattle beasts.' For in this business of peat-cutting there are immemorial usages and rights, and all is accomplished in a seemly, communal manner. Even the distance within which one may approach the neighbouring banks is by a wise custom restricted to a matter of twenty-five yards; though that again is a modern, less romantic rendering of the original law governing the distance, which was as far as a man could throw the 'tuskar'.

The surface having been tirred and the soft black bed of peat exposed, the real business of peat-cutting now begins, and ready hands are gathered round the gaffer and his tuskar; for the tuskar is the very symbol and substance of peat-cutting, with a root deep in the beginnings of speech – a long, straight, stout shaft fixed at the foot into a blade shaped like the letter L, the long arm being called the 'feather,' and the short the 'heel.' It is this blade that conditions the width and thickness of the peat, the size of the blade varying in different parts of the Highlands. The depth (or length) of the peat is equal to the distance between the foot of the blade and a little 'step' that stands out at right angles to the shaft, in all a matter of anything up to eighteen inches. When one end of the bank has been cut, cleared, and exposed to the necessary depth with a spade, the man with the tuskar gets to work. Holding the tuskar upright with the L-shaped blade in position, he puts his foot on the step and sinks the blade straight down till the step touches the surface; then, by jerking the shaft backwards, the blade is levered forward, and tears the peat neatly from its bottom hold. The man at the tuskar's foot (at his post in 'the belly of the bank') catches the peat from the blade and deftly throws it to another, who catches it on the swing and deposits it with a neat thud on the heather. Meantime the tuskar has shifted across the width of the heel (a couple of inches or so), down sinks the blade through this product of decayed vegetation, and a second peat is on the way. Soon the whole process gains a certain rhythm that permits of the peats being handled and thrown with an amazing accuracy and freedom from breakages, several workers taking part in the spreading out; and the ground round about the man with the tuskar becomes a mosaic of oily black peat, through which a finger may be poked with soft ease. Indeed, a wise native, intimate with the styles of local peat-cutters, may pass over the bank many days afterwards, and say with interested certainty, 'I see they hed Geordie o' Jeemags at the tuskar an' Big Daan in the belly.' For there is something about the shape of Geordie's peat that differs from any one else's peat as distinctly as one painter's brush-mark does from another's, while the imprints of Big Daan's thumbs and forefingers are as individual as his calligraphy.

From the direction of a blue wisp of smoke that has been long curling its fragrance upwards there comes at last a shout that is not unwelcome. Backs are straightened, perspiration wiped, stock taken of progress. Work is getting on finely and the day is holding up. There is a quiet satisfaction for the eye travelling over the chequer-board of peat. The promise of fulfilment of a year's necessity is there. Beyond, across a flat boggy 'flow,' the eye comes up against the solid mass of long-backed Scaraben, with, farther up the moor, the peak of Morven rising to a height of 2313 feet, both dominating a natural barrier ridge shutting off, on the south, the Cattachs from the Caithnessmen. Keen eyes pick up small herds of deer, but the protective coloration is so perfect at any distance that only keen, trained eyes can. But it requires no trained faculty to catch the silence, the sense of ageless, brooding immobility, the remote, wind-swept cleanness, the austerity.

Yet geologically the moor has had its dramatic past, just as surely as any transient eye now gazing on its seeming unchangeability; and not only geologically, but humanly too. There is the occasional outcropping of 'bog-oak' or charred remnant of fir, hazel, or other tree, with the tradition that once upon a time vast woods were burnt down in order to expel wolves and other wild animals with which the country was anciently infested; or, alternately, the tradition that the harrowing Danes took a drastic spoiler's interest in creating great forest fires; not to forget the theory of the savage obliged to burn the trunk of the tree which he wished to fell. But apart from that, apart from the geological formation of the peat-bog itself with its extensive distribution over the temperate zone, there are the nearer, more human, weird stories of unique 'finds' at the peat-cutting itself, from the rapt unearthing of vessels of ancient and superbly flavoured usque-baugh to the revealing, with all due mystery and sense of tragedy, of a human body perfectly preserved. There is one rather unusual story concerning the discovery by some of the moor-folk of the trappings of a war-horse. The arresting item in the conclusion is to the effect that the yellow decorative metal of the harness was found to be so comparatively soft that the moormen, to their delight, had little difficulty in cutting and shaping it into eye-holes for their boots! How pleasant a story for the tongue of the advocate of the abolition of the gold standard! Yet the stories that remain most vividly are the fascinating, repellent, creepy boyhood tales of awful moor tragedy, with the memory now as of a haunting, dead, moon-like face in a still tarn.

If the newly cut peats have been favoured with fair drought, two or three weeks should see them ready for 'lifting.' This is the hardest, least varied, most back-aching bit of the whole business. The upper surface of the peat has got sun-and-weather-baked to a firm hardness, but the underside, through contact with the damp heather, is still soft. Wind and sun must get at both sides, so, placing one peat on its long edge, you stand two more on end against it. Without straightening your back you carry on this seemingly endless process, being careful not to break the peats, and yet to give them sufficient stability to withstand the possible ravages of a high wind. Three by three, till the skin on the fingers gets tender and sore from contact with the weather-hardened surfaces. The sigh of relief that sees the last peat on its feet is profound.

More weeks elapse, and the peats, now fairly firm all over, but not yet properly dried throughout, are 'stored' in little mounds, so that the searching wind may whistle through them. As has been indicated, the length of time a peat requires to get into the dry fuel state is conditioned by the weather, and instances there have been where no progress was made beyond the initial cutting, the peats being abandoned to the merciless rain and the sodden bog.

In due course, horse and cart come on the scene to remove the peats from the bank to the roadside, where they are stacked in preparation for the triumphant home-taking.

The building of a peat-stack by the gable-end securely enough to withstand the winter storms, and at the same time to throw off the softening influences of rain and snow, is quite an art in itself. As the carts come home with their loads, the 'goodman' is busy with line and measurement, willing young hands both helping and retarding. For the many comings and goings, the old tradition of a kitchen table ever ready with bread and cheese and a 'dram,' as the occasion's true hospitality is still striven after, but nowadays one of the triumvirate has had a price put on his head and is beginning not to know his homely and age-long brethren.

Standing at last four square to a' the airts, the peat-stack has in its heart all of life and warmth, of hope and geniality, many a bright 'lowe' that will blaze up and flicker uncertain shadows at many a *ceilidh*. Whatever else, in whatever abundance, may have been garnered, how destitute and stricken without that! 'The hearthstone of the Gael,' says the poet. The true symbol!

# White Fishing on the Caithness Coast

*Chambers's Journal*, 1924

A cold wintry morning with a heaving lift in the sea; a sky banked by massive clouds that lower threateningly; a small wind from off the sea with a cutting edge to it; now and again a spot of rain stinging the face. Standing near the point of the old cement pier, one feels there is little romance in this business of going down to the sea in ships – little romance, but plenty of cold, uninviting danger and even more of bitter, hard work. Against the breakwater that forms the opposing wing of this narrow inlet on a wild, precipitous Caithness coast, the long roll of the sea smashes itself to froth, but without warmth – even of passion. The most characteristic quality – a relentless encompassing, sucking cruelty – is exhibited with such deadly indifference that one feels, in a shuddering moment, that if an army of men were drowned there before one's eyes, the insatiable green water would not pause even to lick its chops.

So it breeds the hardy race of men who, as the school-books teach, have had no small hand in making 'our island story.' Running in on the wind – they are favoured today – the brown sails come from the 'haddie ground.' Small boats these, undecked mostly, that pitch and toss like corks on a turbulent river. We wait for the first one to make the narrow opening. Straight on the pier-head she comes, with a certain gallant indifference that mocks the sea and raises a spark of warm admiration in the cold watcher. Now she is at hand, heaved to the crest of every wave, sent sprawling to its trough, but coming, always coming, nose to the pier. At the right moment her head is eased off, she gets the last kick from the wind, and as the block tackle rattles and the traveller slips down the mast, she glides safely alongside the quay.

There is a gathering of folk. Questions are asked and casually answered. 'Ay, there wis a bit lift in id the day ... Weel, aboot three baskets o' haddies an' a basket o' blockies [codling] ... They're gettan scarce.' No more. There is none of the enthusiasm or the despondency of the amateur fisherman here; merely a grave, unemotional attitude born surely out of the element with which these men have been in such close contact since first they 'traiked off as callow school-boys to the cold 'ebb' for a 'baiting' of mussels.

The catch is thrown, each according to a kind, from the open hold into a cran-basket (four such baskets filled with herring make the measure of a cran) and heaved on to the quay. Two of the crew carry it to the little curing station, where the local fishcurer is prepared to receive the contents and deal with them in the most profitable way. Haddock, whiting, cod, codling, coalfish, flounders, and a few odds and ends, from crabs to starfish, make up the catch.

Primarily the fishcurer wants the haddock. But if a boat sells him its total haddock catch he must be prepared to take the codling too. In creeks such as this one, where a direct daily service with the southern markets is not possible, no matter how early the fish be landed, and where, in addition, freightage charges constitute an almost prohibitive burden, the industry in despatching fresh fish is small; for haddock arriving on the market two days old, after having been shaken to a soft, sticky appearance over a long journey, do not command the same sale or price as fish brought to market a few hours after being landed. Codling, however are despatched in boxes without ice (there is none available), and the curer states he is satisfied if he can realise a price sufficient to cover all his charges – though it may confidently be added there is not infrequently a small margin of profit as well.

However, *the* fish is the haddock. And already I notice four or five women entering the curing-shed. They have oilskin aprons on and are obviously ready for their work. The little boats come in one by one – five in all – and the total haddock catch is soon piled up on the benches. The women are now busy gutting, splitting open, and scrubbing the fish in the sweetest (and coldest!) of spring water, preparatory to the interesting process of turning a fresh haddock into an appetising 'finnan.' In many places on the Scottish coast 'smoking haddies' is an important industry, but it can readily be understood that nowhere is its importance so vital as where freightage charges and distance from the markets severely handicap the marketing of fresh fish. In passing, a word may well be said about this industry, though a special article would be necessary to give an adequate outline of its history and of its processes.

The name finnan is popularly believed to be derived from the little village of Findon, on the coast a few miles south of Aberdeen, though authorities seem to agree that finnans were first cured 'near the Findhorn.' Altogether the controversy is somewhat obscure, especially to those old curers and fisher-men who have followed the industry on the Moray Firth. However that may be, the making of the true finnan in the fishing-villages south of Aberdeen was at one time a simple and homely industry, as so many of our old Scottish industries were. The young lass sat by the peat fire knitting. Whilst watching that the fire did not go out she had to be equally careful that it did not blaze up in 'lowes.' In the latter case she damped the flame's ardour with a handful of sawdust. The 'lum reek' did not go straight up the chimney in the ordinary way; instead, the 'lum' or 'chimbley' itself went slantwise across the gable wall, and in its course passed through a specially built cupboard, where the haddies hung by their ears to spars with bent, nail-like hooks. These homely scenes, with whatsoever of human romance entered into them, vanished, as the handloooms vanished before the mills. Now along our coast special curing-sheds deal with quantities of fish not by the cupboardful but by the ton.

Moreover, nowadays the astute nose of a Glasgow or Edinburgh fish-dealer may not be easily deceived. He opens a box of finnans and takes their bouquet. 'Peat!' he will sniff disdainfully, if no wood shaving and oak sawdust have gone to the smoking process; for it is the oak that gives the true and delicate flavour to a smoked haddie. And there are degrees of flavouring. To those who know only the full body of the 'dark-browns' one word of advice: Try the 'light-pales'! Roughly, the light-pale stage is reached thus. After the fish have been finally cleaned and split they are dropped into a tank of brine for about an hour and a half. Thence they are picked out, graded, and pinned by the ears to those thin spars bristling with their rows of nail-like hooks – 'tenterhooks.' When they have been in the smoke long enough to get their tails dry they are about ready.

The rest of the catch from whiting to the possible crab, is shared out amongst the crew for home consumption and for the selling of 'six-pence-worths' to neighbours. But the crab! What a centre of interest to the young of the family, from its powerful claws, its propensity for crawling below kitchen dressers, to the final feast, and the use of the big toes by the very young men as pipes for illicit smoking of 'foug' – that sort of shag produced from rolling and teasing out a piece of mossy peat!

Meantime, the fisherman's day is not done. He has been at sea since the wee sma' hours, for he is one of those who perforce recognise a very literal tide in the affairs of men. All through the bitter cold of the early morning he has been heaved about in the frail shell of his 'small-boat.' Now he has to set about preparing for the following morning, for while the weather lasts every hour is precious. And the preparation of the 'small-line' is the nightmare of all fishermen's lives, ay, and of the lives of their wives and families as well. Each fisherman – and there are almost invariably four or five fishermen to every small-boat – has his small-line, and each small-line for every outing has to be cleaned, baited, shot, and hauled. When it is remembered that a small-line carries about 600 hooks hanging at regular intervals, about a fathom apart, to a correspondingly tremendous length of supporting back-line, the amount of toil involved may be dimly grasped.

So he sets off home with the 'skoo' (a basket specially designed for holding the baited lined) hitched across his back, and the prospect of a cold, busy afternoon looming up in front.

After 'denner' the work begins. The fisherman himself, on a wooden chair out by the back-door if the weather permits, otherwise in the stone-floored kitchen, settles down to the task of 'redding the line.' This consists in running it carefully from end to end through the fingers into an empty cran-basket, cleaning each hook as it comes along, and with a dexterous loop and twist burying its barb in the 'tipping,' which is made of home-twisted strands of horse hair, and which takes the place of the trout fisherman's gut. In the business of taking a 600-hook line from the sea, laden with fish, crustaceans, molluscs, and other strange things of the deep, the marvel to the casual observer may well be that the whole line is not in a hopelessly inextricable tangle. Sometimes, indeed, there is confusion of knots and twists – 'raivels' – and hooks have to be followed through a perfect maze of intersecting coils, but with a good stiff pipe of 'bogie roll' going full blast after a warm, satisfying meal, the patience of the fisherman, at all times great, now seems to be inexhaustible. Hook after hook is fished out, and bit by bit the line passes, smoothly coiled, into the cran-basket. When it is considered that at the rate of even four hooks a minute the whole task would take about two and a half hours, its arduous and painstaking nature may be understood. Moreover, as happens frequently enough, many of the hooks have been torn from their tippings. In such a case the tipping is threaded through the basket, to hang outside until such time as the line has been 'redded' and the 'baiting' is in view. Then a new hook is 'bisked' on with strong thread to the old tipping, or, if the latter has been badly torn, a complete new tipping with hook is affixed.

The line redded, the next question is the getting of bait. Mussel bait is best, though limpets are used when mussels are not available. The limpet, however, is a poor substitute, even when boiled, and it is usually boiled both to soften the bait and to make the 'shelling' easier. (After boiling, it can be easily gouged out with a thumb, but if raw it has to be scooped out with an empty limpet shell, and this is a difficult art, requiring much practice before facility is gained.) If the fisherman has a family of helpers, he will find himself in the lucky position of being able to send one of them to the 'ebb' with a bag to bring home sufficient mussels for a 'baiting.' Unfortunately these mussels are not naturally available on this rocky coast, and have to be 'imported,' generally from Tain, Leith, or England. Those from the Dornoch Firth, near Tain, are dredged from the bottom, are not riddled, and consequently hold on to enough of their native grit and byssus to permit them quickly to anchor themselves when laid out in beds on a suitable tidal shore (the 'ebb'). Those from elsewhere are generally riddled smooth and clean, and are stored in bags within the tidal shore (the 'ebb'). Those from elsewhere are generally riddled smooth and clean, and are stored in bags within the tidal harbour-basin itself.

When sufficient mussels have been dug and plucked from their bed, or simply taken from the sack, the youth hurries home with them. Now begins the shelling process, one in which an astounding degree of proficiency can be, and is, attained. With a sharp knife (the 'corkag,' make for the purpose) the bivalve is cunningly split open, broken over in two, and the bait scooped out plump, whole, and juicy into a bowl. So quickly does the knife work in experienced fingers, that it all seems easy as shelling peas – until tried! And efficiency is never sacrificed to speed, for the bait must reach the bowl perfectly whole and never torn or ragged, otherwise when the head of the house is baiting there will be gentle remarks to make young ears tingle. For it is a point of honour with each fisherman that his line be perfectly baited – slovenly work is a thing not to be borne.

And soon the redded line begins to coil back again into the skoo. As each hook comes along, it is unwound from its tipping and cunningly hidden in a soft, luring mussel-bait. Side by side in rows the baited hooks are placed, the back-line being curled in behind. All must be done with very great care

and precision, so that in the darkness of the following morning, when the small-boat is again tossing to the cold sea, the
line may run out, bait after bait, without a single hitch. And
when the last hook is baited, and the fisherman, straightening
his back, looks at the clock, he finds the following morning is
indeed but a very few hours away.

It is a strenuous life, though interrupted all too frequently by
stormy weather – and long spells of stormy weather mean
poverty. A brave race of men, with quiet, undemonstrative
ways, inured to the hardships of life, and tempered to a fine
self-reliance by the ever-lurking danger in the restless sea. All
their lives long they have known only the sailing-boat, and
now, in face of the concentration of the fishing industry in a
few big ports, such as Wick, Fraserburgh, Aberdeen, and of
the general introduction of steam and motor power, they are a
vanishing race. Even today it is one of the saddest things on
earth to wander down to their little harbours, and to feel the
silence hanging about everything like a shroud; the cooperages
with gaping windows and roofless walls, the jetties crumbling,
the lonely, cavernous crying of the gulls, the few small-boats
even emphasising the loneliness, where once, in the season's
height, 150 two-masted herring-boats thronged, 'mid a life
pulsing with the thousand and one energies of a great
industry. To many a mind not yet past middle age, how
memory will recall the hum of life that was there: the chant to
the creaking halyards as mast or sail went aloft, the gay,
stirring sight of the fleet, one by one, negotiating the narrow
entrance, the children's voices, the clank of the coopers'
hammers, the herring-gutters with their gay chatter and
incredibly dexterous fingers, the guttural Gaelic voices of the
hired men from the Lews ('Lewsachs'), the endless coming and
going, the glamour and glow of abounding life. It is hard to
have to write it, but all has gone gray, and the sadness is
inexpressible. Only the sea pays no attention, but day by day,
with cold indifference, eats a little more of the cement, loosens
a stone here, a stone there, slowly undermines a jetty till it sags
with the decrepitude of decay.

# John o' Groat's

*Chambers's Journal, 1925*

There is a strange fascination for man in the idea of a place which is the end of things. Is not the whole history of world-exploration a history of the human desire to 'compass the ends of the earth'? And not only in the physical realm but in the poetic, too. 'Beyond the horizon's brim' lies the garden of the Hesperides, or the more magical (to A Gael, anyway) *Tir nan Og*, land of the ever-young; 'marvellous land, full of music, where the hair is primrose yellow and the body white as snow ... and the hue of the foxglove is on every cheek.' So to the scientist, mathematician, philosopher – a reaching out to an end, an ultimate. Without as much, how stagnant, sterile, life would be!

Yet so constantly a 'striving and a striving and an ending in nothing' does the ambition prove itself, so often does the end turn to ashes or, at best, be recognised but as the first step in an endless aspiring, that unless man were fronted by some incalculable destiny, surely he would have grown tired of the game long, long ago; grown tired and cynical, and died.

World-old reflections, perhaps, that yet have a certain warmth of life when, for the first time, on a clear sunny day, you top the last ridge of Caithness county and look down on the land of John o'Groat's. In that first glimpse there is something of the magic of at least transient fulfilment, as though desire did at last manage to taste of its own dream. There is the last rim of the mainland, and beyond it the blue, blue sea, and set in the sea surely the Isles of the Blest! Truly a touch of enchantment rendered breathless by a faint incredulity. You turn your back, hoping the human, if mostly foolish, hope that the 'first fine rapture' may be recaptured in a second glimpse – suddenly to find that this gray flat land of Caithness you have been driving through, treeless, stone-diked, or fenced with great slate flags, has magically developed a mysterious charm, a breadth of atmosphere, a wonder of its own, that appeals as old tales of the clans and the Norsemen appeal, as sagas and poems of Ossian. For the prospect is now unquestionably on the grand scale, compelling, magnificent. Indeed, it may well be that from no other spot in these islands can such a sense of illimitable horizons be obtained. A bare four hundred feet above sea level, yet the whole county stretches from your feet like a single moor, till a limit is set to it by Morven, that lodestar of Caithness fishermen, and the Sutherland peaks standing against the horizon like little cones. Southward the eye sweeps the whole extent of the Moray Firth, and imagines it can trace very faintly the dim outlines of the Moray hills on the other side. A complete history of the Moray Firth as a fertile fishing ground, embracing the habits, customs, and dress of the numberless generations of fishermen who have inhabited its creeks and harbours, would, I often think, be as fascinating and romantic a history as could well be written. Eastward the Moray Firth widens, merges, and gets lost in the North Sea, and in a moment the eye is baffled by the meeting of sea and sky in that faint line that is like the closing of mysterious lips. Then, suddenly turning back again, turning northwards, behold the blue waters once more, and the islands of the Orkneys and Stroma isle set in the blue waters!

It is difficult to refrain from phantasy should one happen to look on the Pentland Firth on a day of flying wind and sun. Even on the calmest day the waters are always in turmoil, sweeping their restless tidal way at anything from six to ten miles an hour, west or east, to the raging 'Men of Mey' or to the devouring 'Boars of Duncansby,' those tumultuous collisions of cross currents; but with sun behind one and the wind blowing, how intensely blue the colour, how white the tossing manes of the sea-horses, glistening, gleaming! It becomes easy to see how myth and legend found beginnings, how folk-lore and strange traditions thrived, and, what perhaps appeals more, how beginnings had necessarily to be born out of the stuff of heroism. Lives spent between those surging waters and this gray land had to be cast in a strong mould, and the bards' tales of their heroes, mythical or otherwise, had to be of a nature that inspired to deeds of endurance and courage and daring.

The thought sends the eye of its own accord across the Pentland, seeking nor'-west for the Brough of Birsay, which lies a little to the north of that visible headland of Hoy, standing so starkly there, face to the west. Somewhere off the fatal brough one night in June 1916, in a storm-ridden sea, the *Hampshire* went down .... The bards and the skalds, in the old sense, are dead, perhaps, but the old wonder and fear are still native to the heart, and who knows what 'myth' the historian of a thousand years hence may have to 'explain away'?

So one looks at the islands more curiously. Midway in the channel is the bare but picturesque-looking island of Stroma. It is not one of the Orkney group, and comes under the jurisdiction of the parish of Canisbay, in which John o' Groat's is situated. For any one with a whole day to spend, a row or a sail across (weather being suitable – which, alas! is the exception), and an exploration of the manifold points of interest, make a memorable excursion. Bearing about nor'-east, Skerry Lighthouse flashes in the sun like a white marble column, looking a very fairylike guard this fair day for the 'Stormy Pentland.' Then, stretching right and left, bounding the horizon in front, are the southern Orkneys. Rock-bound they look, raising their walls out of the water not unlike gargantuan battleships, anchored with that gray immobility that suggests titan power. A certain entrance is pointed out to you, the entrance to Scapa Flow. Scapa Flow, the *Hampshire*. ... Suddenly you realise the sheer ancient and modern national importance of this 'end of things.' Galley and Dreadnought, Viking and War Minister: History repeats herself, however dressed for the occasion; the line of endeavour is continuous, and the heroic soul is still the heroic soul.

The famous traditional John o' Groat's House is now nothing but a green mound, and to the present generation the name images little beyond white gleaming sands, where one hunts endless hours for the beautiful 'John o' Groat's buckies,' and the modern hotel with its 'every convenience,' from garage to wine cellar. There is a room in this hotel, which, on your remarking as to its somewhat curious shape, will possibly be the means of calling forth the story of the strange building of that house which is now the green mound, the house that has succeeded in giving its interesting name in perpetuity to this end of the world. The story, or tradition, as I have heard it, varies in the telling, but the generally accepted version is that given, I understand, by Dr Morison in his *Old Statistical Account of Canisbay*. It is a very human story, not without its parallel in more famous corners of world history. Stated briefly, it runs somewhat like this:

Three brothers, natives of Holland, Malcolm, Gavin, and John de Groat, came from the south of Scotland to Caithness during the reign of James IV, with a letter from that Scottish monarch recommending them to the countenance and protection of his loving subjects in the county. They obtained lands in the parish of Canisbay, either by purchase or royal charter, and in the course of time so throve that there came to be eight different proprietors of the name of Groat. To commemorate the date of their arrival in the county they established an annual feast, and on one such festive occasion the inevitable dispute arose on the all-important question of precedence. (Highland enough, these Dutchmen! though not possessing, it appears, the perfect aplomb of the chieftain who, in somewhat similar circumstances, dismissed the matter with the magnificent gesture: 'Wherever the Macpherson sits, that's the head of the table!'). John de Groat, now far on in years, settled what looked like the development of an ugly dispute by the cunningest interference and advice. In a voice full of the wisdom and toleration of the aged, he pointed out how well off they were in matters of worldly gear in this the land of their adoption; how fratricidal strife would leave them open to the attack of their enemies and would inevitably be their undoing;

and how, if they would but behave themselves on the present occasion and go quietly home, he would guarantee them a satisfactory solution of the difficulty at the next meeting (for he was wise enough to know that advice alone rarely achieves human ends).

Having so persuaded them, the worthy John forthwith set about the erection of a house that would have eight walls, eight windows, and eight doors; and when in due course the octagonal house was completed, he placed inside it an oak table with eight sides. At the next meeting each entered by his own door and sat at an unquestionable head of the table; and so enchanted were they all with this most equitable arrangement that the old harmony was restored. Thus, like the Arthurian Round Table, came into existence John o' Groat's House (though it would seem, indeed, the wily Dutchman could have given points to the illustrious knights!).

One other explanation of the name may be given. It is certainly an ingenious one, and mentioned by Robert Mackay in his *History of the House of Mackay* as being traditional, though Calder, the Caithness historian, has been unable to find, he states, any such tradition in the county. Here it is:

John, a ferryman plying between Orkney and Caithness, had frequent disputes with his passengers about the fare, till in the end the magistrates took up the matter and fixed the charge at fourpence, or one *groat*, per head. Thereafter the ferryman was called Johnny Groat, and thus became the ancestor of the whole Groat family.

For devastating simplicity it certainly takes some beating, and if a libel on the house of Groat – or, in other words, a manufactured 'tradition' – it all goes to show that the ways of the heathen Chinee in that which is 'childlike and bland' were not unknown to some derisive clansman bent on putting 'interloping foreigners' in their place!

One further and naïvely irresistible thing about this old house was recorded by the late 'Cairnduna' in one of his interesting northern articles to the *John o'Groat's Journal*, as having been extracted by him from the inside cover of the visitors' book 'kept at an old-world hospice at Huna.' Below a representation of the arms of the Groat family is the date 1839 and some writing, from which the following: 'It is stated in Chambers's *Picture of Scotland*, 3rd edition, volume 2, page 306, that the foundations or ruins of John o' Groat's House, which is perhaps the most celebrated in the whole world, are still to be seen.'

In history of a more or less northern importance the vicinity of John o' Groat's has been necessarily embroiled to a very great extent. Every small ferry in the Highlands has its own local history and traditions, but John o' Groat's represented the landing-spot on the mainland for the Norse Earls of Orkney – was, so to speak, an international ferry. According to a remote tradition it was in striving to reach this spot that the Picts were lost in the Pentland Firth, after having been first driven to the Orkneys by the victorious Scots, and then back again by the Orcadians; whence arose the name itself – Pictland or Pentland Firth. But two historical happenings of a much wider appeal may be mentioned; and for appropriate quotations reference has been made to that admirable *History of Caithness* by Calder (first published, 1861).

The first throws a certain very interesting light on what might be called the brighter side of soldiering under Cromwell, or, to quote Calder, 'Cromwell's soldiers are represented in history as rigid sectaries of the most austere cast, to whom everything in the shape of amusement, and especially on the Lord's day, was a heinous sin and an abomination, but it would seem that such of them at least as came to John o' Groat's were not so very strict.'

He arrives at this conclusion after quoting some entries from the old session record of Canisbay,which would point to an occupation by Cromwellian troops on three separate occasions. The first on 29th March 1652: 'No session holden by reason the Inglishe were quartered in the bounds; the congregation was few in number, and ther was not a sederunt of elders, nather was ther any delinquents.' Again on 2nd May 1652: 'Ther not being a sederunt, by reason of a party of Englishe horsemen being in our fields, whilk made the congregation fewer in number, and severall of the elders to be absent.' And finally, that which gives to so much reading between the lines, on 30th December 1655: 'Adam Seaton convict of drinking on the Sabbathe, and having masking plays in his house for the Inglishe men, he was ordained to make publick confession of his fault next Sabbathe.'

The second instance, which will appeal to students of Scottish history, and perhaps particularly to sympathisers, poetic or otherwise, with the Jacobite cause, has to do with the gallant Montrose. When he crossed over from Orkney with a body of men, it was in the vicinity of John o' Groat's that he landed on that last fateful attempt of his to win a throne for a Stuart. Three flags he unfurled – two for the king, and one of his own, with the motto which so significantly sums up the character of the man – '*Nil Medium.*' Or, to translate it into his own quatrain:

> He either fears his fate too much,
> Or his deserts are small,
> That dares not put it to the touch
> To gain or lose it all.

Montrose lost it all at Carbisdale in the spring of 1650, and fled the stricken field, only to meet his end at the hands of his enemies at the Cross in the High Street of Edinburgh, in a manner surely brutal and heathenish enough to accord ill with their sanctimonious professions.

# Highland Games

*Scots Magazine, 1931*

There is an odd persistence about Highland customs and institutions. We are always doing something to keep them alive, as though they came out of a social past which we cannot let die – or dare not. Searching among the underlying reasons we come on something not so much sentimental as quixotic. There is that air of holding to a tradition of manners which was natural to the knight of La Mancha – and is perhaps not altogether unnatural now to many leaders of the Gaelic 'causes.' Or should one use the more general term and say 'Scottish causes'? Anyway, has not Bernard Shaw said of Cunninghame-Graham that when not in his company he believes the man a myth? When young John MacCormick is holding forth on our parlous state, or Mr Angus Robertson is rounding a period to the honour of the ancient tongue, might not the spectacle appeal to a Scottish Cervantes – with the irony to appreciate what they are tilting at? And if that may seem amusing to the rest of us, it may be as well to remember that his master was sometimes amusing to Sancho Panza, for those of us who dare not lead are proverbially wise.

Well, of all our institutions, Sancho Panza has got complete control of one, namely, our Highland Games. No idealism, false or otherwise, is allowed to intrude there. The race is to the swift and the battle to the strong – for cash. No nonsense about it: a free field and no favour. And so we have our two or three heavy and light athletes travelling from village to village, games to games, and collecting the money that local endeavour is able to gather for them. In a word, it has become for the most part a commercial business. This has disgusted those who have a mind above what they consider professional sport of the worst kind, who still believe in games as a field of local rivalry and disciplined effort with thrilling uncertainty as its climax, and who in their beliefs, quixotic or unconscious, derive from an age anterior to the time of Christ. For the Highland Games go far back into Gaelic legend, and at least we know of one Boy Corps that competed in friendly rivalry in all field sports, in honour and chivalry, of whose splendid company, Cuchulainn, that small dark man, was one. Against such a conception, Sancho Panza and his travelling 'weights' of many kinds, do not make an impressive show. The more the pity, for there has persisted – there persists still – in our Highland Games an elusive semblance of its ancient meaning.

But it grows less and less, for commerce in sport always gathers about it a certain amount of wangling and cynicism, and sorry enough stories must inevitably follow in the wake of a hard-working professionalism. But without conjuring up the shady or ludicrous side, let us consider for a moment a simple little 'difficulty' that occurred the other day. It is the custom for the piper who pulls off the major prizes to pipe for the dancing. On this occasion when the dancers were called, the piper appeared in a blue suit and bowler hat. The judge, astonished, called him over and enquired what this rig-out meant. And the piper explained that as he wanted to catch an early train he thought he would save time by changing his clothes before he started piping for the dancing. He had collected all the money in quick time and now he wanted to 'beat it' at the earliest moment in the bowler hat of decency. The man's unconscious attitude (and he was a good piper) to kilt and bonnet may rouse certain humorous and even illuminating reflections! All the brave show of the ancient garb was become a condition in the cash-winning game, a piece of ritualism which an otherwise sensible and decent man had got to observe – though hardly to the extent of imperilling the catching of an early train. The judge, however, thought otherwise and in lucid terms returned the hero to his tent. And afterwards, the theme being upon him, the judge referred us to the spectacle on the field of the heavyweights who have to wear the kilt. Almost to a man each wore an obliterating overcoat and had a cap's snout more or less over one ear, not to mention what was characterised as a ' filthy sweater' round one burly neck.

Now even if it were granted that this matter of dress is not important, still it does at least indicate to the discerning the natural attitude of professionalism towards our Highland Games. These travelling athletes are for the most part splendid fellows. Let it be clearly understood that there is no aspersion cast upon them personally. All we are trying to do here is to realise exactly what today's Highland Games stand for and what they call into being.

Assuming, then, that the Highland Games have got their distinctive note from the perpetuation of an old tradition, it would seem reasonable, if it is desired that the unique note be kept, to continue as far as possible the spirit of that tradition. Now, as I see it, that means concentration on the local aspect of the event. The whole endeavour should be to stimulate Highland music, athletics, and dancing within the district where the Games are held. The reasons are clear. Country life, particularly in these days of intense emigration of the finest stock and the consequent creation of an atmosphere of defeat and decay, needs all the healthy stimulation it can get. Athletics, music, and dancing breed sound bodies, active minds, and a distinct social sense. All that grows sour and inferior in the inaction of hopelessness gets routed out of the system by a fine rivalry. The schoolboy hopes someday to emulate the athletic deeds of his elder whom (and this is the significant part) he meets, and talks to, and secretly admires, and whom he may see any night 'having a practice' ; or if his mind runs to music, then he has countless opportunities of listening to the local champion and gaining for his own use by imperceptible degrees that appreciation of the finer shades of execution which is about all that technique means. It is impossible to overestimate the importance of this. It gets at the core not merely of the Games, but of the whole conception of communal life. It shows us the real value of tradition, shows us growing and blossoming from our own roots. (The old Gaelic heroes were of the people, doing the day's tasks about steading or shore.) Without this tradition we may live, but season by season we throw less of the flower and finally become fruitless and settling into inevitable decay.

Now there are two direct ways of looking at that local aspect. One can say frankly that one does not believe in it; or, believing in it, that it is no longer possible to achieve.

If one does not believe in it, then let us by all means have our perambulating professionals lifting the local cash. And let *piobaireachd* (though why perpetuate so exclusively Highland a musical form?) be set to competition in bowler hats. Only, to be logical, one should drop the description 'Highland Games' and get an apter label. In this case, however, there would never be the excitement attending a horse race or 'the dogs,' because it is already known who is going to win. The three 'heavy' visitors, for example, have already competed and will compete times out of mind. We know who will be first, second, and third, beyond a peradventure. We are thus done out of the fun of even a modest bet. Finally, if we attend the exhibition at all, it is in the end for lack of anything better to do.

If, alternatively, one does not bow to this 'open' logic, yet believes it impossible to achieve the local aims, then possibly the only honest thing to do is to let the whole sorry business go by the board.

There is, however, the middle way, the way of compromise, and this is where the local secretary or organiser becomes impatient of the critic. Without having the 'big names,' he asserts, there will be no gate money, the Games will not be a 'success.' Yet he is satisfied he provides for all local enthusiasm by having local events, in which outsiders are not allowed to compete. He thus presents us with the spectacle of the open, and the rivalry of the local, competitions, a double performance. What more could man desire?

Now admittedly this is not an easy position, and if we enquire into our secretary's reasoning, let it be understood that it is done with every sympathy. The application of purely destructive criticism has become nowadays too common (because alas too easy) in this land of ours.

In the first place, then, we find that the big prizes go to the open events. It would thus appear on the face of it that the main aim is to draw the small professional group. It is here definitely suggested that that aim is bad and that it arises out of the fundamentally wrong attitude. Straightway the local events take on a diminished and often amusing appearance. No matter how well the local competitors do, their performance is subject to a running comparison and commentary. They feel they are competing on a lower plane and their whole mental aspect is affected accordingly. The spirit they might bring to the healthy questing for local championships is vitiated by comparison with their athletic superiors, whose sole reason for attendance is to collect money. It has accordingly come to pass that at the end of the day your local competitor is now not concerned with what he has done so much as with what amount he has 'lifted.' The cynicism underlying this is bad for sport and worse for the arts of music and dancing. The net result is that your more sensitive local spirits do not compete at all, the whole affair takes on a certain air of disrepute, and the true object of bringing out the communal best, with victory more important than the prize, is defeated.

Lay all the emphasis and organisation on local effort, spend most of the money that can be raised on providing attractive local prizes, let there be cups or medals or badges for distinction or honour, let the whole affair be fostered again from however simple if true beginnings, let communal pride enter in from parents to school children, and there would arise a new and more healthy interest in our ancient Highland Games. What is needed is not a blind acceptance of bad conditions, but the initiative to work out new conditions. Let me give an example that came under my own notice not so long ago at a remote village Games. The visiting professionals and the local men had had their usual somewhat unexciting round of events when all at once there descended upon the field some eight or nine youths mounted on motor cycles, each with a young lady posted behind. In the centre of the ring were flags – one less than the number of machines. The ring master began beating the big drum. The motor bikes started round the ring. Whenever the drum stopped the young men drew up their machines and their ladies rushed for the flags. After each rush one squire and his lady had to retire. So it went on; a kind of 'musical chairs' or, if you like, a knightly tournament in miniature, but with the ladies taking active part! Certainly it was by far and away the most attractive and exciting event of the day. Clearly no professionalism entered into this. But consider for a moment the implications, so far as youth and communal excitement and belief in their ways of life are concerned. It was like a new confidence introduced into a dying body. These young men, finding a livelihood in the district, had no inferiority complex either to the starred professionals or to the visitors with southern collars. That does not say that we need applaud the innovation of motor bikes! What is indicated is how important is the spirit in this matter and how significant the whole for the enrichment of country life.

Now it may be considered that there has been shown here no appreciation of the prowess of what we have called the 'visiting professional.' That is entirely to misconstrue my contention. I consider on the contrary that it would be a good thing for the local men to see the man who is the champion of his class. But this could easily be arranged by simply inviting him at a fee to attend to 'give an exhibition.' And while this might be advisable on the athletic side, I should say that it would be essential on the piping and dancing side. To have a master of *ceòl mór* play at a given time would be the local way of honouring the master and the occasion. There would be no feeling of the local men competing against him. You would thus obtain the 'draw' that the secretary desires and at the same time let the local aspirant see the highest development of his secret dream. As for the 'masters,' they would themselves compete in the two or three great national gatherings (such as 'The Northern Meetings' in Inverness) where their claims to leadership could be openly settled.

In some such way the evils of an insidious professionalism might be combated and renewed life and interest given to the local Games. Not that any more than the mere fringe of the subject has here been touched upon. If it were possible to renew the belief in ourselves, in our Scottish past and culture, I should like to envisage something far greater than has ever yet been attempted, something of pageantry and colour that would quicken the spirit and give to its pride and gaiety an expressive and memorable form. But as the Highland Games have declined in aim and repute, so it is being alleged we as a people have fallen from our ancient high estate, and in that case I am afraid it would require more than a tinkering with the ways of professional sport to put us where we rightly belong. But that is perhaps the beginning of another story.

# The Ferry of the Dead

*Scots Magazine, 1937*

'In the main the Celts, after advancing to the West of Europe, retreated in the same direction. If we look carefully at the map we shall see that the districts where they are found are refuges. The Celts came to a stop there at the sea, clinging to the rocks. Beyond the sea was their next world. They stayed on the shore, waiting for the ferry, like the dead in Procopios.... What now remains of the Celts, in the west of their ancient dominion, was driven there and confined there by other peoples arriving or growing up behind them. This general movement of expansion and contraction taking the Celts to the west and confining them there may be called the law of Celticism. It must be studied as a capital fact of European history.'*

Is it possible, by a careful analysis of the existing conditions of the Gaelic people of Scotland, to dispute the continuing validity of this 'law of Celticism'? Can we suggest that the long historic process, like a ninth wave, has reached not an ultimate shore where it breaks and dies but an ultimate rock of endurance which, taking the force of the wave, sends it backward?

It might be pleasant to think that we could, not merely for the sake of the Highlands but for what might be added to the diminishing goodwill of the world. For if we take such a manifestation of the Celtic spirit as our annual Mod we find there social and spiritual values that could be of a deep and regenerating potency. It is essentially a festival of the folk and

* *The Rise of the Celts* (Henri Hubert)

calls into being the true communal virtues: hospitality, gaiety, singing, colour, dancing, in an atmosphere of goodfellowship where, for the time being, worldliness with its greedy gains and losses is forgotten. And it is founded on a historical reality: the ceilidh-house, the house where folk met and discussed the affairs of the day, of yesterday, and of legendary times, and illustrated their friendliness by epic or epigram, song or weird story, for the common interest or laughter: a clearing-house not of banknotes or cheques but of those imponderable debts of the spirit that humanity still owes itself but is forgetting how to pay.

Of the reality of this Celtic attitude to life there can be little doubt. What actuates the Mod is the ancient profound spirit of fellowship, of communism, a desire for human warmth and entertainment and instruction in a circle of social equality. So much was this the case in the past that the privacy of the home never became 'the castle' (that hangover of feudalism in whose irony the common Englishman is smothered). Privacy was all the more delicately respected and misfortune assisted because the front door of hospitality was never locked. It was all a way of living, of life. And the Mod is a festival we have based on it.

And so we arrive at the point where we have to ask ourselves a few questions and endeavour to answer them honestly.

Is this way of life still a reality? Is the old order of crofting and sea-fishing still fruitfully continuing or is it 'clinging to the rocks ... waiting for the ferry ...'? Has it lost its self-sufficiency, its independence, and how now does it diminishingly continue to survive, on what substance or charities or doles? What sort of spirit actuates it? How fares it with its language?

Is the law of Celticism working here with a cumulative inevitability, a final swiftness, visible to us almost from month to month? And if it is, what in essence is this Mod? A pure manifestation of nostalgia? A bath of sentimentality? Something of which the sensitive Gael, who believes he knows the true native conditions, may be a little shy and ashamed when he has not the toughness to enjoy the merry-go-round while it lasts and then forget it?

For many recent weeks I have been wandering around the West and North. For a generation I have known the conditions of life in this region fairly intimately and have been able therefore, perhaps, to assess the value of official statistics giving the figures of decline in population and in Gaelic-speaking, coincident with an increase in lunacy and public or State assistance. One can, for example, discuss with a school-master, minister, priest, or other well-informed resident, the chances of survival of a specific crofting area or fishing creek and arrive at fairly sound conclusions. Where a township is inhabited by the old, by bachelors or spinsters; and the young who, in the ordinary course of nature, should have inherited the crofts and reared families have departed for the cities or emigrated; then, in the absence of claimants for the land from outside crofting areas, what is going to happen is quite clear; for the very same processes have already been at work in other townships, where the land has gone out of cultivation and become part of a sheep farm or of a sporting estate (for I discovered a process going on of large estates in the West getting broken up into small estates, whose owners, wanting their land for sporting purposes, get rid of the sheep-farmer, who, as a tenant with none of the rights of the crofter, must on due notice sell out and go).

Again in the fishing creeks one finds a similar sort of process going on. In these columns last month I mentioned some of my experiences with fishermen or those interested in sea-fishing as an industry. Here the matter is directly affected by outside agencies like trawlers and foreign markets, and there is little good in blinking the fact that for the most part the western Gael is making no effort to hold his own at sea. Trawler-men think of him not as a sea-fighter or even a land-fighter but as a mouth-fighter. 'Another Highland grouse.' 'He wants money for nothing.' They are ironic, sarcastic.

Take a magnificently situated seaport like Oban, with direct railway service to Glasgow and with good fishing grounds in the neighbouring seas, and compare it with any of the small ports on the Moray Firth like Lossiemouth, Buckie, Hopeman, or even the remote village creeks like Lybster or

Scrabster, and you will be forced to find some sort of excuse for the absence of local boats in the West compared with their multiplicity in the East. Why in the Caledonian Canal is it always East Coast boats you encounter going to or coming from the West? Why are there not at least a dozen seine-net boats based on Oban (where there is surely enough capital to finance a small fleet of them) that would not only prosecute their own local fishings but go farther afield, like the Lossiemouth seine-netter I recently ran into in the Caledonian Canal, returning from Ayr after a fairly profitable season? Why in the name of simple enterprise should one be forced in Kinlochbervie or the Lews to buy white fish from Aberdeen?

It was not always like that, and for sheer sea-knowledge and craft of sailing, the real seaman of the Isles could not be beaten. In the old days when they caught their ling and cod from the Tiree bank to the Flannans and split and dried them on their western rocks, there was no hardier breed of men alive. Nor had they any aid from outside, then; no pension or dole: on the contrary, they had to fight for what at the best was a hard existence against the rapacity of their landlords, whose exactions, as in kelp-burning, or savagery, as in the clearances, makes one wonder how the Gael of East or West continues to pay respect to chiefship. Yet in these days the ceilidh was a reality, where music fulfilled its true function and where oral literature and the social graces gave life some meaning and communal purpose.

While writing this, one particular island in the far West came to mind. It is a small island, yet a generation ago had no less than thirty fishing boats sailing from its bay. Today it has none. Now the population has not declined – an unusual fact, I recognise. Fishing for and dry-curing ling was the important or money part of its sea industry, though, of course, herring and most kinds of white fish were caught in their season. Fish and oil from fish livers were part of a diet, simple, perhaps, but at least now known to contain all the essential vitamins.

Well, there is an old seaman in that bay who has a good boat and would like to start fishing again. With him will die the knowledge of where the fishing banks lie and he would like to pass on that knowledge before it is too late. A man from that district, who is making money in a professional career elsewhere, offered as a gift to fit out the boat with everything necessary in the way of gear if the old man could get a crew of young fellows to go to sea with him. And the old man tried – but without success. Why? Because the young fellows were on the dole or qualifying for the dole and would not lose the certainties thereof for the uncertainties of the sea. They would not even 'give it a trial' lest their neighbours should 'tell on them.' Yet there is a home market for white fish in that particular part of the world that never existed in the old days.

I have satisfied myself that this is not only a true story but that it is more or less typical. It is now a saying that the Islesman knows the Unemployment Insurance Acts better than his Bible, and there is a joke in Lewis to the effect that a man of a certain district will not go to a funeral unless he gets an insurance stamp. The number of cases that have to be officially investigated of what is called 'faked employment' is beginning to present a real problem to the Departments concerned. This is now so widely known that commercial travellers out West while away an evening hour in relating the more ingenious methods of gathering insurance stamps as a new kind of smoke-room story.

It would be easy to give in detail typical instances of employment deliberately constructed to pass the test of being insurable work within the meaning of the Unemployment Insurance Acts, but that would take up too much space; and, in any case, I am more anxious to consider criticism, aired in the press, which has made use of terms like moral degradation. For the kernel of the trouble lies in this, that these Acts were designed for industrial areas and not for the Highlands and Islands, and that accordingly the Highlander finds himself naturally impelled so to reconstruct his circumstances as to bring them within the scope of the Acts. Occasional employment outside the croft has always been a feature of life either for himself or one or more of his family. Take the case of a man who has had several months of continuous or intermittent road work and at the end of it finds himself with twenty stamps on his card. These stamps represent lost money to him – unless he can within two years increase their total to thirty, when he will be in a position to claim unemployment insurance benefit and, in due course, the benefits that follow on. (And public assistance is now losing the old dreadful stigma of parish pauperdom.) In that man's position I naturally should make every effort to get my thirty stamps. If, therefore, a few of us could arrange a scheme of work to meet our needs and in the process enter into such contracts of service with one another as would satisfy the Acts, what official or other person has the right to inquire into the necessity for the work or raise any moral issue whatsoever? Because a man is an Old Age Pensioner, that does not preclude his becoming an employer of labour. You may think he has not the money? Nowadays an Old Age Pensioner can have a few hundred pounds behind him or he may have a son in Canada – and, in any case, what concern is that of yours? But the work is palpably unnecessary and would never have been undertaken but for … Who are you to judge another's necessity? Stick to the terms of your Acts of Parliament and investigate my case as searchingly as you like, but within these terms – and keep your moral judgments to butter your good salary.

An old man approaches me, now happily drawing my dole, to go to sea with him. He can offer me no guarantee that I'll make as much money as I at present get weekly for doing nothing, for he is not going to pay me a wage, he is merely going to share out what our problematic catches may realise after a portion has been retained for boat and gear. Sea-work, especially in the wintertime, can be the most dangerous and gruelling employment in the world. Any sort of land job is easier and infinitely more comfortable. Besides, we know how the trawlers have cleared up the banks. I make excuses to the old man and am relieved when he turns away to try someone else.

Nor is it any use telling me that this sort of behaviour kills initiative, destroys the ancient virtues of self-reliance and independence. No doubt. But, for that matter of it, what initiative can a man show who lives on a salary and carries out the routine of, say, a Government office? Initiative is the one thing he must not have. Perfect routine achieves perfect efficiency, in the office as in the factory. And as for the man who draws his living from dividends or rents, his particular sort of initiative, if any, never applies to the sphere of real work. As for self-reliance and independence – you keep your eye on your boss.

Now I do not wish all this to be understood as a complete picture of life in Scottish Gaeldom. Far from it. There are folk who work hard and never draw the dole, just as there are crofting areas vastly overcrowded, while the ancient ways of courtesy and independence are still to be found. But the decline in crofting and sea-fishing and the increase in State aid are facts that must be realised, for they indicate a change in every feature of the social scene, from the use of tinned foods to cheap finery, that is surely taking place and that will presently make the Mod about as meaningful and pleasant a piece of pageantry as dancing round the maypole.

In Old Age, Widows', &c., Pensions (contributory and non-contributory) it is estimated that something like £1500 a week goes into Lewis alone, and over £700 from Army Pensions. If to that be added the amounts paid out in the dole, in health insurance benefits, in public assistance, and even in crofting grants in one form or other from the Department of Agriculture, the total must represent a very considerable weekly sum for a population of 25,000.

But even this business of direct State aid must in time decrease, as the old die, the population continues to decline, and even the opportunities for constructing employment within the meaning of the Acts grow inevitably fewer. In a recent annual report, the Medical Officer of Health for the whole county of Ross stated that the population was becoming increasingly old and that the age distribution had left the normal. The death rate was over 16 per 1000, the birth rate 14, while there had been an increase of 2 per cent in those over 65 in the last census period.

So it would seem that in fact M. Hubert's 'law of Celticism' is duly working itself out. The busiest ferry on the West is the ferry to Iona and those who use it go to commune with the dead.

That is the broad aspect of things as I see them. But we are masters of our destiny to some degree. It is bad legislation to apply Acts designed for one sphere of social activity to quite another kind of sphere. Trawling can be stopped. Fishing could be made lucrative for the fishermen. Proper transport, co-operative marketing, controlled prices, and other constructive features discussed by us all *ad nauseam,* are not beyond human realisation. But I am not concerned with the constructive aspect for the moment. I am concerned only with the realities, with trying to see clearly and objectively things as they are. And when I turn to the Mod and try to see what it is doing for Gaeldom, I find it difficult to be impressed. Despite its concern with the things of the spirit, it is essentially neither a creative body nor an inspiration towards creation. At the core, it stands for the remembrance of things past, and does not envisage a future in terms of that past. Its most notable leaders or publicists deprecate action of any kind.

I remember a talk with one of them who had made a magnificent rhetorical speech on the glories of Gaeldom to an admiring audience. But when, later, we tried to get him, in face of the material realities, to formulate some scheme of action whereby the glories might continue to be fed and housed, and thereby naturally perpetuated in the future, his reply was that he would have nothing to do with politics. The Mod must remain pure and undefiled. Actually he feared realist action. He was too pleased with things as they are. For in this show he was a figure. His personal prestige was warmed by his own rhetoric, and, for the rest, his sons had got the right English accent. Someone mentioned what Ireland had done. He walked away. Ireland, indeed! We, who had made the British Empire!

And that is why no real Gael, in his heart, believes in the Mod. And when he is a decent man he is troubled, because here in truth are precious things of the spirit, and he knows that the life that bred them is dying.

# 'Gentlemen – The Tourist!'

## The New Highland Toast

*Scots Magazine, 1937*

Tourist traffic is becoming a matter of importance in the affairs of most nations, and generally there is a department or semi-official body ready to hand out pamphlets to allure the traveller. Even the intricate matter of money exchange may to a slight extent be manipulated in favour of the visitor as anyone contemplating a tour in Germany should know. The underlying idea is the apparently simple one that money brought into a country and spent there adds to the wealth of that country.

Apparently simple – because this business of the wealth of a country is in reality extremely complex. I got my first lesson here when as a lad I read 'Progress and Poverty' – and learned that in proportion as the wealth of a nation increased so did poverty amidst the workers of that nation. It seemed a mad paradox, but facts proved it true. With this phenomenon most of our modern economists have been concerned, whether of the orthodox kind that rule our banks or of the revolutionary kind like Douglas and Marx. The increase in recent years in unemployment in this country has been accompanied by an increase in the national wealth and by an incalculable increase in the potential national wealth. And the reason for this is simple enough: the perfecting of machinery by invention and scientific discovery at once increases production and displaces labour. That fact is now generally admitted, and the political fight is concentrated on the nature of the remedy required. We are not concerned here with the nature of the remedy, but we are concerned with the underlying facts.

For in the Highlands at the moment a fight is going on over the question of whether or not a limited liability company should be given statutory powers to use the waters of a certain area of a county for the production, by hydro-electricity, of a commercial commodity within that county. The inevitable questions of local rights or jealousies do not concern us here. What is pertinent to our purpose is that prominent opponents of this water-power scheme base their general opposition on two points: (1) they do not desire to see the water power of the Highlands used in creating private industry, and (2) they consider that the tourist traffic should solve all the economic ills of the Highlands.

Now this is a matter of grave, perhaps of crucial, importance to the Highlands at this particular moment in time. For the decline in every phase of Highland life is becoming alarming. It is easy to quote census figures showing a progressive depopulation of the Highland counties, but it is not so easy to grasp precisely what that implies by way of emigration of the youthful best, and the leaving behind of an ever-preponderating number of the aged and unfit. The old croft is no longer a self-supporting unit. The sea-fisheries are in desperate straits. There have been more economic tragedies on the Moray Firth coast in recent years than should last a whole sea-faring nation for a century. The distribution of national or public relief has been constantly increasing, until at last a problem has arisen, particularly in the Outer Isles, that the Department of Health is finding it difficult to solve: the problem of the 'manufacture' of work by men and women, so that, within the meaning of the Act, they may get thirty stamps affixed to a card and so qualify for the dole. The suggestion that one should 'blame' them for this is merely a piece of insufferable moralism. But there is the picture. All vital statistics of the Highlands point the same way. And not least those of insanity.

A correspondent in these pages last month referred to the increase in the inmates of the Inverness District Asylum, which serves the counties of Inverness, Ross, Sutherland, Moray and Nairn. Not only is the pauper lunacy rate for this area far higher than for any other part of Scotland, but it is more than

twice as high as that for the congested industrial towns of
Lanark, where conditions amongst the vast mass of the poor
have been and are surely dreadful enough. The General Board
of Control in its report on pauper lunacy in Scotland states:
'At the top of the list stands without a break the whole
Highland and insular region of Scotland.'

And the Scottish Committee of the British Medical Association, in its Memorandum of Evidence, comments thus: 'One
causative factor is depopulation, which has drained the Highlands and Islands of much good stock, leaving behind weaker
and older people who are unable to stand up to the strain of
daily life on the sea coast or among the hills. Nothing has been
done by way of a really serious attempt to preserve the fine
type of people, mentally and physically, which the Highlands
and Islands have hitherto possessed and produced.'

But the decline of what we call our Highland heritage is
even more marked on – if I may be allowed the phrase – the
cultural side. We may have the finest folk music in the world,
and, in the Gaelic, one of the finest folk literatures. Is any
music being created today, or any literature of the slightest
significance? And what about Gaelic itself? Dying steadily.

Now, painting this negative side is not pleasant. None of us
likes evidence of 'gloom'. The Highlander, despite all writing
to the contrary, is a cheerful fellow. But then so is the con-
sumptive. In short, whether we are made uncomfortable or
not, whether our pride is hurt or not, we must face up to facts
so long as we are truly concerned about the future of our land.
If we are no longer so concerned, then nothing matters but the
self-induced warmth of make-believe until the feast or the
famine is over and the bones left for the inevitable antiquary.

Taking then the Highlands as we know them today, can the
tourist industry in fact restore the economic life of the people,
can it revive what have so long been its whole way of living,
namely crofting and sea-fishing?

First let us revert to our opening remarks. Tourists who
come to this country do spend money. That money, let us say,
increases national wealth. But how far does this tourist money
as spent in the Highlands increase the wealth of the working

Highlander? Could we, as in 'Progress and Poverty,' have an increase of apparent wealth floating about the Highlands coincident with an actual impoverishment of the crofter and fisherman? In short: (1) how does the tourist traffic directly affect the general industries of crofting and sea-fishing, and (2) in how far are the hotels which tourists patronise dependent on the products of Highland labour?

Let me take a certain wide area of the Caithness coast which I visited a few weeks ago. Many townships are there; many scores of crofts. There is a harbour that in its heyday had over a hundred fishing boats sailing from it and now has five motor boats. There is the usual hotel, though not a sporting one. Most of the folk I know personally. The highway to John o' Groat's passes through this region. I went into the matter closely. In this whole area there are two families that benefit, to a certain degree, from the tourist traffic: the family that runs the hotel and the family that runs the garage. No other families benefit. The tourist traffic has not given rise even to one small standing order for fish or for croft produce. That is the fact, and I could analyse it out into minute detail, if space permitted. I could show, for example, what precisely sea-fishing means in the way of capital costs, gear, catches, contracts, and markets, and how tourism cannot even begin to affect it. All through the winter months these boats have been seine-netting for flat fish or haddock – one of their main seasons, when tourists are as remote as swallows. I was there in January, when the recent gales were at their height. For two days and nights the fishermen had not been to bed; they had been standing by their boats, waiting to do what they could, should the next sea tear all the moorings before it. The condition of the inadequate harbour was an unspeakable disgrace to the authorities concerned. And now in the mad seas the old breakwater was going, and already wooden piles could be seen heeling over in the white surf of the bay.

While waiting there, word came to us of a boat having been smashed in a neighbouring creek. Almost certainly it would not have been insured, as insurance rates are prohibitively high to these men struggling so magnificently to make simple

ends meet. The scene was unforgettable. I remember leaving
the harbour once in the half-dark, and, on coming to the main
road, the wind whistling in my ears, having to leap for the
ditch as a magnificent saloon car swept by, bearing the motto
: 'Monte Carlo Rally.' It may have been a moment for ironic
comment. It is sufficient for my purpose to suggest that the
incident adequately illustrates the effect of Highland tourist
traffic on the deep-sea fishing of our coastal creeks and ports.

And as with that Caithness region so with nearly all the rest
of the truly crofting and sea-fishing areas of the Highlands.
Individual houses here and there may be encountered along
the great main roads where a night's accommodation can be
obtained, and in a few special areas, as in Badenoch, there is a
regular house-letting business, run for the most part by
women who otherwise have only slender means of support.
But I am concerned here with the true crofting and fishing
areas, with the crofter and fisherman who have their own
homes and their own families, and my experience satisfies me
that the three months' tourist season does not affect one per
cent of them to the value of one pound sterling.

Now for the hotels, particularly as we know them in the
West, complete with sporting privileges. I suggest that the
food for these hotels is purchased not from local shops or
other local source, but direct from the great city stores,
wholesale or retail. In fact, in view of the table that has to be
provided for high-paying guests, this must be done. The hotel
proprietor has no option. Such fresh foods as milk or vegeta-
bles he generally takes care to provide from his own byre or
garden. And as for sea fish, he keeps in touch with the nearest
town or provides it himself. Last year a friend of mine, staying
in a West Coast hotel, went for a day's sea-fishing in the hotel
boat and helped to swell a very considerable catch. For this
privilege he was charged thirty shillings.

These hotels, in the season, give employment to some maid
servants and gillies, and wages got in this way over a month or
two may affect the economy of a few fishing or crofting
families. But I suggest the effect over all is negligible. Most of
the money drawn at the hotels goes to pay Southern stores,

and the profit retained by the hotel-keeper finds profitable investment neither in crofting nor in sea-fishing.

Tourist traffic, then, as we know it at present, offers no solution of the land and sea problems of the Highlands. Nor can I see how it ever will. True, we can begin to speculate, to imagine crofters' houses trebled in size and furnished with hot and cold water for summer letting. The dreaming of such kailyaird dreams is a simple matter. To Highlanders, particularly if they are well-to-do and living south of the line, this seems a favourite pastime. Nor am I concerned here with the type that a complete or swarming tourism would inevitably breed. I could hardly trust my pen to dilate on this matter. I am too conscious of the greatness that has been bred out of our Highland land and sea in the past. I see too clearly these fishermen, drenched in storm-spray, standing quietly by their boats two days and two nights. Their harbours going derelict, while landlord and county council and Government refuse responsibility in turn. Foreign trawlers out in the Firth, where British trawlers are prohibited, swinging round a central anchor on a three-mile radius and sweeping the bottom of the sea clean as a kitchen floor before their eyes. Brave men, fighting a losing battle with unending courage, a battle to them not, as we might poetically think, against elemental forces, but against the far more grisly force of debt. They have no money to build harbours or compel economic marketing. The week before the storm one of these boats had sent twenty-six boxes of haddocks to the South market – over a ton of food from the finest of fishing grounds – and had got back, after transport and other charges had been met, exactly twenty-six shillings.

Yes, it is easy to dream dreams and to draw up schemes; to see the harbours rebuilt, new boats purchased, cheap transport, co-operative marketing, Government action against trawlers and Government co-ordination of the whole industry, with control of seine and ring netting and care for spawning grounds. It is easy to launch out, in imagination, on increased afforestation, local industries such as fish-freezing, fish-canning, cloth-weaving, kelp-burning, eggs and honey; to assist crofting, with all the power supplied by small hydro-electric plants – on the basis, say, of one plant to one glen, so that there would be no more jealousies! I myself have been turning over that dream for a generation. And at least it is a decent dream that might well perpetuate and make creative once more the Highland spirit.

But alas! I see no slightest sign of such a dream ever being realised. The Government at Westminster cares nothing for it; is overwhelmed in any case by economic distress on a vaster scale elsewhere. And as for our local authorities – such a conception of things does not appear to have come even within their dreams. The best the Inverness Town Council could suggest the other night at a public meeting was tourism as the solution of all our ills, and the Highlands no longer as a brain or a heart or a creative force but as 'a lung' – a lung freed from all taint of industrialism, so that folk from south of the Highland line could clamber into its emptiness to breathe.

Well, it is not enough. In face of the realities of the situation I find it impossible, for example, to blame the Lochaber men who want work and believe they can find it in the proposed factories of the Caledonian power scheme. This may be re-mote from the ideal – but who in authority is going to bother about the ideal in their lifetime? If I were an unemployed man in the Highlands, a broken fisherman, a three-months gillie, I should prefer to work in a factory in the Highlands rather than in one in Lanarkshire, South Wales or the Midlands of Eng-land. The folk who object to the scheme because it is to be run for private profit would not impress me, because each one of them runs his own business for private profit. Even their objection on the basis that it would destroy the tourist traffic I should see to be specious, inasmuch as countries like Switzer-land, Norway, and Sweden, with hydro-electric works all over them, have an immense tourist traffic; and even in the Irish Free State, since the erection of the Shannon scheme (in the most lovely part of the country), with its pylons marching across the breadth of Ireland, tourism has increased enor-mously.

But tourism one way or the other wouldn't matter. I should

demand a man's work, and I should demand it in my own land. I might hate the forces, national or local, that had so misgoverned and impoverished the Highlands as to compel me away from my fishing or crofting and into a factory. But better a factory than starvation; better a self-respecting worker in my own trade union than a half-sycophant depending on the whims of a passing tourist. For I should know that so long as Highlandmen are employed in the Highlands, so long as they constitute the mass of the workers there, then there is hope for the Highlands. In virile life, however employed, there is a future, because free men will not bear indefinitely the evils of our present industrial system. But when this free virile life is absent, then not all the deserving old women attending to all the tourists of the world and prattling of the scenic beauty of empty glens can save the ancient heritage from decay and death.

# My Bit of Britain

*The Field, 1941*

To one who has wandered about the Highlands of Scotland most of his life, it is difficult all in a moment to say, 'This is my favourite bit.' After a long spell on the East Coast, to go by Invermoriston and Loch Cluanie to the shores of Loch Duich is to emerge into a new world that the blood knows as immemorially old. On the treeless plain of Caithness, one can see the pines in the gorge on the way to Gairloch; by the gaunt rock-bound shores of the north-east, the islands and anchorages in the Western Ocean. Once in a reckless moment I bought a boat, and, with the help of Admiralty charts and the grace of God, we navigated her – my wife and I – along much of that western seaboard during summer months of distinctly varied weather. It was an experience to dream about. We often do.

Perhaps the deciding factor in this matter of choice is an irrational one, irrational in the sense that it has little to do with any scheme of preference involving explicit aesthetic or material considerations. This is my corner of the Highlands, here my earliest memories were formed, and so, for better or for worse, richer or poorer, I stick by it. It is the way the blood argues. And in itself it is perhaps not a bad way, for it springs out of affection and loyalty. All the theorists who argue so nobly against nationalism and for peace miss this simple point, it seems to me. When the blood fondly says 'This is my land,' it is at that moment profoundly in harmony and at peace. When it cannot say that, something has gone wrong, and it is that something that is the evil thing.

Not, of course, that I think my bit is inferior to any other in its variety of natural feature and attractiveness! The country that lies around the borders of the counties of Caithness and Sutherland provides, in fact, more striking scenic contrasts than I have found elsewhere throughout our island. Approaching Caithness along the north road, you leave behind a land of heather and mountain, the great mass of Ben Hope, the airy granite peaks of Ben Laoghal, and then suddenly the eye encounters the vast rolling plain of Caithness. Behind is a memory of little croft houses backed by heather; in front are farms whose fences are upended flagstones, whose very pattern seems bare, rectangular, austere, like certain modernist pictures. With the sun in the south – and despite southern opinion it does shine quite often in this northland – the waters of the Pentland Firth take on a vivid brilliant blue, and in this blue the Orkneys lie at anchor like fabulous battleships. Here lived the ancient native Pict, and hither came the Gaelic missionary to woo him from his Druidism, and the Viking raider to despoil him of land and life.

Those of us who live, or have lived, in cities, and know modern industrialism in all its phases, may justly feel some impatience at useless echoes of battles long ago. But this northland is not an industrial area and must live as best it can amid its own influences. When I was a boy, that unique circular edifice called a broch was one corner of a wide playground. I say unique because it is unknown outside Scotland, and, inside Scotland, Caithness has the greatest number. They are now ruins, of course – some of them were ruins overgrown with moss when the Vikings came in the eighth or ninth century – but our ruin still had its beehive chamber intact in the twelve-foot thick wall. There we admired the cunning masonry, cut our names on the stone, or dug up shells of edible shellfish.

The south road to this area skirts the shores of the North Sea until it runs into the fishing creek of Helmsdale, the outlet of the Strath of Kildonan. Thence it climbs steeply, in great hairpin loops round ravines, to the Ord of Caithness, where the sea cliffs are over 600 feet high. From this elevated primeval moorland, where no habitation is, the coastline is seen as a continuous wall of rock to distant Clyth Ness. Actually there are a few short gaps in this wall, and each is – or was – a fishing creek. Indeed, if we are interested in the lives of a people, in economic issues, we have here before us a perfect example of the beginning, rise, and fall of a very great industry, all within a century, last century.

When we look at the sea off our coasts it is normally impossible to tell which way the tide is running, it is even difficult to tell whether the tide is flowing or ebbing without studying the actual beach at our feet for some time. But in the Pentland Firth you can see the tidal stream running east or west, you can see its beginnings, its increase, its height, when it is like a gigantic and turbulent river, its decline and fall to slack water. In cities or industrial areas it may be difficult to say with certainty how the economic current is flowing, but here on the Caithness coast a whole tidal process in economics can be studied from beginning to end.

It is a remarkable story. Early in last century the Government decided that the herring fisheries along our coasts – hitherto a monopoly of the Dutch – should be nationally encouraged, and with that object in view offered to pay a bounty of at first two shillings and then four on every barrel of herring cured. Round about the time Napoleon was being convoyed to St. Helena, the herring tide set in along these northern shores. Every kind of craft was pressed into service, local boat-building was, as we now say, geared to an ever-increasing output, coopers were trained, curing yards built, women and girls of the crofts became expert gutters and packers, and soon there was discernible that hectic movement of life we associate with a gold rush. In 1830 the bounties were dropped, but by then nothing could stop the progress of the industry and it took the loss of the bounties in its stride. Schooners appeared to carry the barrels to distant lands. The Baltic markets in particular became a northern gold mine. From these creeks in that rock wall – Helmsdale, Dunbeath, Lybster, Clyth – hundreds of boats were fishing. The boats increased in size, grew in numbers. As time went on, they took in the West Coast fishing, the season at the Shetlands, at Fraserburgh and Peterhead, and finally set sail for East Anglia. Then came steam, the large ports with docking facilities and unlimited capital, and the golden age of the creeks began to decline. By the early years of this century, they were derelict.

One more economic note and the living pattern of this region in recent generations may be seen. For what immediately preceded, and for some time coincided with, the growth of the herring fisheries pertained to the land and was as horrible in destruction as the rise of the fisheries was remarkable in construction. This was the movement by the great landlords of clearing the crofters out of the glens in order to make room for sheep. In that area which goes up the Strath of Kildonan from Helmsdale and on to the Pentland Firth some 15,000 crofters were dispossessed and driven from their homes, often in circumstances of brutality. Great numbers of them were shipped abroad, but many joined the fishing communities on the coast, and their descendants today, as in the last war, man our mine-sweepers and fighting craft, for where expert seamanship and individual initiative are needed, there they are naturally found.

So in this far northland, if we may not know much of the life of cities and industrial areas, we know all right what the struggle for existence means. The land and the sea, the produce of earth and ocean: these have been the concern of the folk who live on the crofts and in the fishing villages. They bred a fine tough type when the going was good; daring men, willing to lay hands on opportunity, prepared to face anything, quietly religious.

With the coming of the motor-engined fishing boat, around forty feet keel, there has been a small stirring of life in some of the creeks. But whether this seaboard will ever again see the tumultuous life it once knew is another matter. Some of us have our theories, but optimism is not a quality that finds over-ready houseroom here where men and women have known what struggle means.

Between the two seas is a vast hinterland of mountain, moor, and glen, given over to sheep, grouse, and deer, for the

vast bulk of the folk live by or near the sea. It is good sporting
country, and many a happy day I have spent in its wilds. As I
write, one holiday in particular comes back to mind. I owned
at the time a small saloon car whose seats were so arranged
that in a couple of minutes they could be extended into two
beds. There are many ways of sleeping out. I have done it in an
old bothy, under a strip of canvas, or openly in the heather
without any covering (this last way would be as good as any,
did not the midges delight in tangling themselves in your hair).
But for the comfort that is perfect, I have never known
anything to equal that little saloon car. After an exhausting
expedition on foot, to return and eat, to put up a fishing rod
and get a few trout in the evening, to have a last stroll to some
particular eminence or hollow, to wander back and, while the
beds are being prepared, to get some fresh water in the kettle,
to undress and get into bed, to pour out two drinks for careful
dilution from the kettle's spout, to light a last cigarette, to lie
back and watch the night come in and around in a slow
quietude, is to know why man needed and so created the word
'magic.'

We were in the heart of a deer forest, many miles from the
nearest house, which was a stalker's. We had neither rifle nor
gun and so got on terms of intimacy with the wild life of the
region. We could, for example, look at a young mountain hare
and say, 'His top speed is 26 m.p.h.,' for we occasionally did
a long cruise for milk and bread and so could test such
matters, as no hare would leave the road in front until he came
to his own home path, not though we almost sat on his tail.
Sometimes, in a ground mist, for fear of running him down, I
would stop the car. But presently we would come on him
again, for he had rested as we had rested, and then, with one
ear forward and one aft, he would show us his paces once
more. In this way one seemed to get a sort of intuitive
knowledge of the home or social life of the hare. But the social
life of the deer had now and then a fascination which I will not
attempt to describe. For we were no students of wild life. We
were there to enjoy what we saw, not only in wild life, but in
the shapes of hills and corries and moors, in loch and stream,

and, over all, in the ever-varying effects of sun and shadow and mist and small rain. But that hour of summer twilight, when all our world grew quiet, gathered all the hours into it, as a man's life is gathered in his thought. For the rest, let it be said that we did have a particular interest (for such an interest gives cohesion to a holiday) – my wife in what plant life could be found, and myself in the sources of one or two streams.

Physically the two counties are divided by a range of hills which, though not very high (Morven, 2,313ft. is the highest peak) are made particularly prominent by the general flatness of Caithness. There is a road that runs from Latheron on the North Sea to Thurso on the Pentland Firth across some twenty-five miles of moorland, from which this range looks in certain lights like a vast bastion of mountain. But the quality of the light on the Caithness moors is sometimes of an extraordinary fineness. It is not altogether a matter of great distances, for I know the moor of Rannoch at all hours, and have looked over wide enough vistas in some Continental countries. Perhaps the clear air of these northern latitudes and the surrounding seas may have something to do with it – not to mention the effect of countless square miles of ling turned to pale gold.

But this land, which guide books ignore, beyond a reference to bare, treeless, and uninteresting, has its intimate beauty in its little glens or straths. Scenery in the public sense has its fashions, of course, and some of us are not impressed unless the mountains rear perilously overhead and the glens are deep as Gehenna. We must be shocked into taking notice. Even death must be on a colossal scale before we are impressed. But as an intimate affair, death, like life and like beauty, is individual and personal. The death of a true friend still touches us more nearly than the death of a thousand strangers. If it doesn't, something is going wrong.

These small straths, like the Strath of Dunbeath, have this intimate beauty. In boyhood we get to know every square yard of it. We encompass it physically and our memories hold it. Birches, hazel trees for nutting, pools with trout and an occasionally visible salmon, river-flats with the wind on the bracken and disappearing rabbit scuts, a wealth of wild flower and small bird life, the soaring hawk, the unexpected roe, the ancient graveyard, thoughts of the folk who once lived far inland in straths and hollows, the past and the present held in a moment of day-dream.

There may be a lot of nostalgia in the Canadian boatman's longing for the 'lone shieling' and the 'misty island,' but at least it springs from memories that had once held this intimacy and beauty, in moments beyond the hazards and struggles of life, and would experience it again if it could.

# High Summer by a Mountain Lochan

*Scotland's Magazine, 1960*

Even a picture postcard of a Highland scene can trigger off so many associations that the mind is everywhere it has ever been in the wild Highlands at once. That is probably why hotels sell so many of them; or why we are arrested when we come upon a particularly fine camera study in a magazine. Critics who may not have the associations (and do not care for picture postcards anyhow) may wryly suggest, for example, that the blue of the loch is a bit too good to be true; but, to those who know, the blue may not be quite good enough, may not have that vivid intensity which at the unexpected moment stops one's breath. The blue is alive, it is incredible. At that point, sitting down is a gift, for the sheer physical labour of getting there has worked the everyday humours out of the flesh, and the mind at last is free of time and space.

From its new angle the eye now finds the hills beyond the loch and they look flattened, for summer sunlight has this effect. They drowse in peace as if they had knuckled their height under them, as a Highland cow does or a stag. Mile upon square mile, until the blue is caught again on remote horizons vaguely but sufficiently to distinguish it from the sky. Lost in looking, one hears the silence, and gradually becomes aware that the silence is not just an absence of sound, but something positive in itself.

The treacherous mists, the winter storms, the terror, the shelter stones – they are buried so deep now that they are forgotten; but who knows how much they enrich the peace, the silence, the feeling of ineffable well-being? Only those with enough experience could tell us – if it can be told.

# Nationalism and Internationalism

*Scots Magazine, 1931*

The other day I happened to meet a Scottish painter and etcher who was kind enough to invite me to a private view of some of his recent work. It was distinguished work, full of vision, and aware of all the ways of the moderns, but by no means the least interesting part of my visit was the artist's own ideas and experiences elicited by, let me hope, natural questions. For example, a couple of his canvases were concerned with ploughed fields. The serpentine furrow was the motif in a bare Scottish landscape. Not, possibly, what would popularly be called a 'picture.' Yet the artist had been intimately attracted by the subject, and, though believing that the attraction was peculiar and personal, had nonetheless had it included in a group of subjects from different parts of the world for a one-man show. Consider his surprise when the bare furrows caught the particular attention of the metropolitan dealers. It was almost enough to make him conclude that trips to North Africa may be fascinating, but not necessarily essential for the production of masterpieces! And if this theme provided a nearly endless one for speculation at least the one fact had emerged, namely, that by the artist's doing what he knew intimately, and what had appealed to him deeply in his own country, he had attracted the closest attention of art lovers in other countries.

I mention this experience because it happens to be the most recent of many that have, from time to time, seemed to explain to me the relationship of nationalism to internationalism. Nationalism creates that which internationalism enjoys. The more varied and multiple your nationalism, the richer and profounder your internationalism. Conversely, where the nation would disappear and the world become a single body governed by the same machinery of laws and ideas, the common stock of culture would tend to become uniform and static. For cosmopolitanism does not readily breed the intense vision or rebellion of the native or individual spirit. On the contrary, its natural attitude is to deplore it as being unnecessary, often wasteful, and nearly always in bad form. Cosmopolitanism working through this man-of-the-world conception might out of an ultimate logic create its own ideal, but it would be the deathly or neutral idea of the perfection of the beehive.

Now the question arises here: – Why, then, is there in the world of affairs today the idea of antagonism between nationalism and internationalism? If internationalism is nationality's flower, why war? And it is precisely in this awful region of war that so many of us lose our bearings. For nationalism breeds patriotism; patriotism, it is asserted, breeds antagonism; and antagonism needs the mailed fist.

But patriotism, as a true emotion, is full of life; it has kinship with poetry and music and none with destruction and death. From the earliest times it has been the world's singing subject. In the history of each nation it has been a unifying and precious possession. Each nation has been prepared to fight for it, when it would not quite have been prepared to fight for its music and poetry, or, indeed, for any other of the mind's preoccupations except religion. Patriotism, indeed, fed such arts as poetry and music. Possibly no other single emotion is more responsible for the creation of the world's culture.

But that sort of patriotism has as little to do with jingoism as music has with a factory siren. And it would be almost as reasonable to suggest that we could get rid of the unwelcome noise of our machine age by first of all abolishing musical scales and musical instruments as it would be to suggest that we could get rid of jingoism by first of all abolishing patriotism. There is no philosophic basis here, and the reasoning is of the kind that has been prolific of so much action, or rather

restriction, in recent world legislation. What interferes with
our natural love of country today may regulate our drink to-
morrow, our clothes the day after, and our conjugal relations
next year. Patriotism may yet keep us from being slaves – if
only of the Wellsian aseptic city-honeycombs.

Patriotism (even already the word is beginning to have a
false note) is founded in tradition, and we can no more get
away from tradition than from ourselves. Indeed, immediately
we get away from tradition we do get away from ourselves. A
nation's traditions are the natural inspirations of its people.
How much the child is the product of heredity and how much
of environment may be a debatable point, but that he is the
product of both is unquestionable. Out of his environment,
acted upon by a traditional or national unity, he creates most
profoundly. And to create is to cause or give delight. In the
pure conception of patriotism there is pure pleasure just as
there is in any true function of the arts. And it is only when a
man is moved by the traditions and music and poetry of his
own land that he is in a position to comprehend those of any
other land, for already he has the eyes of sympathy and the
ears of understanding.

How then has patriotism in idea got debauched by war?
Simply because in time of war patriotism is so strongly roused
to protect its frontiers that it has been confounded with the
cause of war. Nations are the natural units in the war game,
just as the family is the natural unit in the nation. But it would
be as ridiculous to destroy our natural unities in the hope of
destroying the war game as it would be to remove our teeth in
the hope of getting rid of a pain caused by our stomachs. For,
as has been said, patriotism is never a cause of war, but is
merely used by war, just as other emotions are, only more
profoundly. For even when nations group into compact em-
pires or into scattered commonwealths, when they lose their
nationhood and traditions, war can still use them. War can use
them without patriotism. War can enjoy the spectacle of patriots
of the same nation fighting each other. War is insatiable, and in
the last resort cares nothing for nations. It cares only for destruc-

tion, and the earth laid waste would be its final triumph.

Why then blame this creative emotion of love of country as causing war, when we have at long last been forced to learn that war is caused by emotions quite other in origin and aim? We know something now of the appallingly defective system of producing and distributing the goods of life that obtains in the world to-day. Men of goodwill and of all political faiths are being staggered at the dreadful paradox of unemployment, hunger, disease, slums – as a result of over-production. Because we have produced more than we need, we are in danger of starvation! At least the spate of war books has made one thing clear (and particularly the German books), that the peoples themselves had no desire for war, that they feared and hated it as it continued, and that in the largest countries in Europe they smashed their own governing machines in the hope of getting some sanity, some food, and a little peace in their time.

Internationalism carried to its logical conclusion of a single centralisation of all power – arms, finance, law-making – could result in the greatest tyranny the mind of man is capable of conceiving. While the nation is still the unit (and history has shown the small unit to be singularly important – consider Greece and Palestine) the individual factor comes into play, and in a myriad personal contacts the finer elements of humanism are retained and tyranny suffered briefly, if at all. But when the governing machine becomes single in control, remote in place, and absolute in power, then hope of reform or progress – which generally means the breaking of an existing mould – would not have the heart to become articulate. Standardisation would be the keyword not only in the material things of life, but also in the spiritual. And whenever conditions got too desperate it would mean revolution, or world war on a basis of class hatred.

The small nation has always been humanity's last bulwark for the individual against that machine, for personal expression against impersonal tyranny, for the quick freedom of the spirit against the flattening steam-roller of mass. It is concerned for the intangible things called its heritage, its beliefs and arts, its distinctive institutions, for everything, in fact, that expresses it. And expression finally implies spirit in an act of creation, which is to say, culture.

Culture thus emerges in the nation, is the nation's flower. Each nation cultivates its own natural flower. The more varieties, the more surprise and pleasure for all. For nationalism in the only sense that matters is not jealous, any more than music is jealous. On the contrary, if we are gardeners or musicians we are anxious to meet gardeners or musicians of other lands and rejoice when their blooms are exquisitely different from our own. In this way life becomes enriched, and contrast is set up as a delight and an inspiration. To have no longer these means for discrimination, to lose the charm that unending variety gives, to miss the spur in the shadow of difference, 'is, on this short day of frost and sun, to sleep before evening.'

# Preserving the Scottish Tongue:
# A Legacy and How to Use It

## Scots Magazine, 1935

*'If I desired to make a testamentary bequest of the income of a sum of £2,000, to be applied to keep up an interest in the knowledge of Scots Vernacular, what would be the most satisfactory form of application?'*

This question was put to the editor of the *Scots Magazine*, J. B. Salmond, who decided to refer it to several notable Scots who he considered were qualified to express an opinion on the matter. Among those consulted were Professor H. J. C. Grierson, Dr John Malcolm Bulloch, George Blake, Dr William Grant, Lewis Spence, Neil M. Gunn, William Harvey, Christine Orr, David Rorie, Hon. Elizabeth Forbes-Sempill, with C. M. Grieve/Hugh MacDiarmid surprisingly absent from the group. The following is Neil M. Gunn's contribution. (ed.)

Unlike Communism or other social creed or manifestation, the Scots Vernacular is an affair exclusively Scottish, and to keep it alive, Scotland must be kept alive. For if Scotland dies, then not only the Vernacular but everything that gives her separate meaning and identity dies with her. In looking therefore for something to keep the Vernacular alive, I should look for whatever body existed with the object of keeping Scotland the nation alive. If no such body existed, then I should know that any concern of mine to finance the Vernacular would be purely antiquarian and of no living value whatsoever.

The logic of this is to me unavoidable. Whenever the conception of the nation is reborn, immediately everything that distinguishes that nation is reborn, including in particular its forms of expression. Take such diverse countries as Norway, Czechoslovakia, and the Irish Free State. In each case when nationhood was resumed, the native language or languages, long fallen into desuetude, became the active concern of the whole people. That is the fact, whether we like to honour it or not.

I know that all this points to the Scottish National Party as the home for the bequest, and to the dread word politics! I cannot help that. I am concerned here only with the honest logic of the business, and logic says it is futile to attempt to stimulate any part of the body when the whole is giving up the ghost.

Let it be admitted, even for the fun of it, that with the Scottish National Party it would be a gamble, but at least it would be a real gamble; and it is just conceivable that a man might feel, here or hereafter, that once in his life he had made a gesture, none the less glorious because it had been both adventurous and hardheaded! But as with the Vernacular, so with the adventurous spirit: it is dying. We want to play safe in a little way. Instead of the living word on our lips, we want the dead word in a dictionary.

# The Myth of the Canny Scot

*Unpublished [1938], National Library of Scotland*

There is a curious myth abroad in the world about the Scot, and it has been suggested, perhaps by his enemies, that it is high time that it was investigated and blown sky-high. It is quite a romantic myth, for it shows the Scotsman as a hard-bitten, hard-headed, canny man, lacking in a sense of humour, fond of adding one dollar to another and sticking to the lot, and sceptical of rash enterprises and adventure of any kind. If ever he does manage to perpetrate a joke, it is always so dry in flavour that it never gives any change away. In fact, he is never going to give anything away at any time if he can possibly help it.

That is roughly the picture. Added to it, of course, are certain virtues of endurance, good business, reliability and guts, but these are correctly commercial assets of which any employer – when the Scot is compelled to have an employer – wisely takes full advantage.

Now who perpetrated this picture, for that it is a complete disguise of the real truth will be shown presently? Some say the English did it, on the principle that it is always sound business to give a dog a doubtful reputation – when one is rather frightened of the dog. And, taking history by and large, there were occasions when the English had every reason to be frightened; when they were, in fact, bitten pretty badly. In truth, the mutual snapping and biting went on so long that at last both English and Scots decided to run their countries more or less as one show. But two partners do not lose their respective characters merely because they join forces in a business deal. So the one partner tries to hang on to his own importance by drawing a picture of the other fellow – that is peculiar.

It is just possible, however, that this may do the Englishman a wrong. It is just possible that the picture was drawn in the first instance by the Scot himself. Why? Because the Scot had such an impossible history to live down.

For the cold sober truth is that the history of Scotland is the most romantic, the most incredible, of any country in Europe. Whenever a venture appeared to be a forlorn hope, a lost cause, there were the Scots battling for it. Whenever it was possible for the Scots to stand in their own material light, they did so with fanatic zeal. An adventure that, if unsuccessful, would mean death and destruction, had always a particular appeal for them. Consider, for example, the groups of clansmen that gathered round that fugitive, Prince Charles Edward Stuart, and set off from their wild bare hills to conquer all Britain and set him up as its king in London. And how nearly they succeeded! – and would have succeeded entirely, if the canny English Jacobites hadn't got cold feet. But back they had to march to Culloden, above the town of Inverness, and on that bloody moor they were wiped out. It was the last battle fought on British soil, and you can see the graves of the clansmen there to this day. And after that battle, death and destruction were let loose on the Highlands with a ferocity of which history, mercifully, has few examples. But did the disillusioned Scots, knowing how they had been misled, damn Prince Charles Edward Stuart? Not a bit of it. On the contrary, they took him to their hearts, called him Bonnie Prince Charlie, and made songs about him, which they sing to this day. That's the sort of wild, hopeless, mad, romantic people the Scots have always shown themselves to be.

And however far back you go, you find the same thing. Here is an instance that is peculiarly apt to the condition of the world today, our world of increasing dictatorships. Yet it occurred in the year 1320 A.D. You will find the words, about to be quoted, in a Declaration to the Pope made by the representatives of what is explicitly called the 'whole community of the Kingdom of Scotland'. In this Declaration they accept Robert the Bruce, the victor of Bannockburn, as their king, but only, they make clear, for so long as he continues to behave himself as their leader. Immediately he shows any signs of selling their freedom, they will at once depose him and put another king in his place. And they will do this, as they phrase it – 'so long as an hundred Scotsmen remain alive'. And then comes the magnificent statement: 'It is not for glory, riches and honours we fight, but only for liberty which no good man loseth but with his life'. And they wrote these words, not before but *after* they had acted on them, after they had fought for them and won the right to express them. And they were expressed over six hundred years ago. Perhaps one may be pardoned for wondering whether any modern democracy would care today to stand uncompromisingly for a declaration in such austere relentless terms. It was a Scots poet of that period who summed up the spirit of his time in the immortal line, 'Freedom is a noble thing'.

Admittedly it is very sad having to blow up the myth of the canny self-seeking Scot in this way. But just as the police office has records of the criminal, so history has the records of the Scot all neatly documented, and he can't get away from them. Even his famous women tended to behave in a manner that was anything but orthodox or canny. It is a moment for the expression of deep regret, but – take Mary Stuart, Mary Queen of Scots. Was there ever a beauty who behaved more incalculably? She did not merely upset men, she upset whole nations, she upset whole churches. All the human passions gathered around her like bees round a honey pot. At last Queen Elizabeth of England – canny Queen Bess – managed to get her shut up in an English prison. But even in prison, where she lay for nineteen long years, that lovely and tragic queen continued to move the unstable hearts of men. Until at last poor Queen Bess was goaded into having her executed. Queen Bess duly died and was buried, but Mary Stuart still lives, like Helen of Troy.

Or take *the* national hero, Wallace. Did ever a more real hero walk the stage of history? His exploits are utterly fantastic in their daring and courage. His life was a thriller that a modern writer couldn't conceive – and, even if he could conceive it, he wouldn't dare write it, because no one would believe him. And the point again that has to be made is that Wallace didn't do these tremendous feats for any good they would bring himself. In fact, whenever he started out, at that very moment, he lost everything he possessed. He did them all for Scotland. And his final reward was that of being hanged, drawn and quartered in London town.

What about the Church? At least the Scot showed himself a quiet simple God-fearing man with nothing to say beyond his prayers – and they were long enough? Again, alas, the picture is wrong. Once the Scot decided to run his Church himself, he did it with a thoroughness that is equalled in our time only by the Russian Revolution. That is no rhetorical statement. Analyse the constitution of the Scottish Church and you will find it based on the Kirk Session. Now a Kirk Session is a small group of management, composed of both clerical and lay members, and its job is to run the kirk or church. It is, in short, a soviet; and the whole Church right up to its great annual meeting or General Assembly is a replica in the religious world of Russia's Soviet system in the political. Or should that have been put the other way round? But perhaps it would be inadvisable to push the parallel – particularly to the extent of suggesting that Lenin got a few tips from the Scottish Church. Enough if the parallelism suggests that Scottish churchmen of old, like the redoubtable and fearless John Knox, were governed by anything but canniness. They liked nothing better than signing a Covenant of freedom, and, when opposed from that same old London town, they duly girded up their loins and went forth and fought for their Covenant, and died for it. In all Scotland's wars she never fought for money or possessions or any material thing. She always fought for some quaint abstract thing like freedom, and promptly ruined herself in the process. When individual Scotsmen wanted to fight for money or position or similar advantage, they had to go abroad. And even then they carried their headlong spendthrift folly with them. There is no other way of explaining the proverb in the

Norwegian tongue, which, translated, means, 'generous as a Scot'; and the common French one, *fier comme un écossais*, – 'proud as a Scot'.

And then to cap the incalculable absurdity of this mad race, we find that the man they worship today, above all others, is not a national liberator like Wallace, not a fighting hero, not a romantic figure like Bonnie Prince Charlie, not a churchman, not an engineer or educationist or hard-boiled go-getter; he is, of all things, a poet. A poet who wrote the finest love songs in the world. A man full of warmth of humanity, who manifestly never counted the cost of any step he ever took. A peasant, born out of the Scottish soil, independent, full of devastating satire for all hypocrisy and meanness, who turned his misfortunes into deathless lyrics, and stated his democratic faith in the words, 'The rank is but the guinea stamp, the man's the gold for all that'. Surely if a man ever lived who blew the myth of the canny Scot to smithereens it was Robert Burns. They toast him annually at Burns Clubs all the world over, in that canny innocuous national beverage called Scotch.

But if you want to get a real slant on this strange myth of the canny Scot, have a look at his incredible country. For the immediate purpose here, three spots may be chosen: a Hebridean Island, Edinburgh the capital, and Glasgow the industrial centre.

Last year, 20,000 visitors from all parts of the world paid homage to Iona. Every year, for fourteen hundred years, thousands of pilgrims have visited that little island of the West Coast of Scotland. For it was there that St. Columba and his brethren lived and worked and from there in their own Gaelic tongue and in Latin, they carried the message of Christianity into pagan places. It is an island full of light and quietude. As one wanders among the ancient ruins, time stands still. There is no spot surely in all the world where man feels more instantly the reality of his own individual soul. No mechanism here, no success, no vanities, no pomp. The long Atlantic rollers break on the snow-white sands. The sea-birds cry. A fisherman works his lines in the Sound. The small cultivated fields round the crofters' cottages are a patchwork of colours.

Peace and quiet and timelessness. All these Hebridean Islands
have this quality of peace and light. The atmospheric and sea
colours are ever varying. The land of the lone shieling on the
misty island. A land with a language and music of its own.
Immemorial and haunting.

To Edinburgh, the capital, with its Princes Street, the finest
street in Europe; and its 'royal mile' extending from
Holyroodhouse to the famous Castle on its rock. What history
has traversed that mile, what dramas of pomp and power,
fightings and hangings, treacheries and nobilities, kings,
queens, murderers, statesmen, churchmen, rebels, through
centuries of greatness and splendour and defeat. Here surely
has passed one of the longest and most startlingly varied and
brilliant of all the pageants of man.

To Glasgow, that was once a small beautiful town on an
innocent little stream. Then the Scots fury got going, and
dredged the little stream, and dammed it, and docked it, until
it became the greatest shipbuilding river in the world, and this
year launched the heaviest thing ever created by the hand of
man, the steamship *Queen Elizabeth.*

The Scottish land, like the Scottish character, is full of these
remarkable contrasts. There is never anything canny in the
Scottish landscape. It is lovely or desperate or intimate or
withdrawn, but never ordinary for very long.

And so we come back to the myth of the canny Scot. Now
he had his neighbours, the English, who had always a sound
eye to the main chance, a canny acquisitive people as their
history shows. He had his allies, the French, who have never
failed to appreciate the good things of life, as *their* history
shows. Did it dawn on him at last that it was high time that he
also began to give heed to the material things and to try to lay
up a little treasure for himself here on earth? No other
explanation suggests itself. And so you can see the naturally
wild headlong fellow doing his best, though obviously not yet
used to his irksome disguise of being canny and dour and
careful. For a man does not leave his origins, his background,
his traditions behind him merely by assuming a disguise.

# Memories of the Months

## A Balance Sheet

### Scots Magazine, 1941

Looking back now on a twelvemonth of these articles, I wonder if they have held any virtue for the casual reader; at the best there can only have been a momentary picture here, a glimpse there, of what happens in the natural world around us in the cycle of a year. Yet if bird, or upland, or wild flower, or falling leaf was for one moment isolated so that object and percipient became one, withdrawn from all else, then something would have been achieved that has been the concern of philosophers throughout the ages!

Withdrawn from all else – there is the snag. For a curious thing is happening to the individual in these days. So drawn together are we in fatality that when the individual breaks free from the concerns of the mass, even for a moment, he is affected by something like a sense of guilt. To turn to Nature is to turn away from the dread realities that encompass us, is to escape, and in the act we suspect a weakness, a selfish trifling, which is highly reprehensible and of which we are openly or secretly ashamed. Almost it seems a pretty, effeminate thing to do, and a robust manliness deplores it, not always without derision.

The war is not altogether responsible for this attitude. It has emphasised it, brought it actively into consciousness, but the whole trend of our age was already shaping that way. To one feverishly engaged in revolutionary politics and anti-pathetic to the present war, for example, the direction of energy towards a calm contemplation of the countryside seems as incongruous as the fiddling that went on while Rome burned.

For a man to be concerned with his own soul, even with his own reactions, is inept, incredible, laughable. There is no time for all that any more, no time for falling leaves in a world falling in ruins. The big business man feels the same way, for his business has got linked up with the business of the State into a mystical wholeness in which all individuals must pull as one; no trouble, no sectional claims, only one united endeavour. Scientists are satisfied that the individual has no immortal soul, and our greatest publicists declare that the only immortal spirit is the immortal spirit of the race. And if final proof were wanted of the prevalence of this attitude, one need only glance at the declarations and actions of the dictators who, for instance, prohibit the individual on pain of death from listening to a foreign broadcast. The ideal is no longer the unity of the individual but the unity of the herd, and advanced thinkers are already contemplating the emergence of a new kind of consciousness, a corporate consciousness of the herd.

Well, we must take our stand somewhere, and for me, quite simply, all this is the great modern heresy. It is an implicit denial of the freedom of the adventuring individual spirit; ideally it is an effort, in time of great difficulty and danger, amid a destructive welter of conflicting ideas, to round man up and drive him back into a state of stable security, such as the security of the beehive, with its perfect economic efficiency and corporate consciousness. It is essentially retrograde, and in the unconscious may perhaps be aligned with the occasional hankering back of the unhappy individual towards a pre-natal security. It is understandable, but the elevation of it into a new faith, however formulated – and it will be inevitably formulated as 'progress' by psychological necessity – is a danger that, I feel, the conscious adventuring individual must fight. But he does not fight with weapons, with the manipulation of mass emotion: he can fight only by standing on his two feet and looking at a thing, at a leaf, a bird, at a new thought, and realising what is taking place in this calm moment of well-being. For this is the moment of unconscious defiance, of the repudiation of the herd in all its tyrannical and bloody ways. Suppress such moments, and the tyranny of the herd, directed by a few individuals (always individuals!) debauched by the will to power, will have become supreme,

Do not let us exaggerate this matter, not even take violent sides, but as calmly as may be consider it reasonably. There is no intention here to deny the high virtues of social life, of society. On the contrary we can never express deeply enough our gratitude for what society has given us: our traditions, our tongue, learning, art, science. Society holds as treasure the best that man in his generations has created. When I listen in to a symphony by turning a knob on my wireless set I have to thank society in a myriad ways for this manifestation of itself as the repository of science and engineering and the arts. And indeed I do, for to be able in a remote country dwelling to listen to an orchestra playing a superb symphony is more than a privilege, it is a marvel of delight. The bellowing of cows in the field, the stamping of horses about the steading, the crying of a few wandering curlew over the roof, take on a more friendly sound in consequence. Life is not only heightened, it is also mellowed, and, where difficult from hardship or mono-tony, it is made more endurable. All that is very true, but what I must take special care not to forget is the symphony itself, which was composed not by society but by an individual.

We cannot conceive of a symphony being composed by society. True, units of that society, working to a pattern like a machine, might be able mathematically to group given themes and variations into a whole, but even that would imply a considerable amount of individual initiative and directive force, and at best the result would be *ersatz*. Whenever society elects to produce only *ersatz* symphony, at that moment individual inspiration will have died, as it has died in the beehive.

I cannot see how we can get away from this. It is either true or it is untrue, and, if true, then the recognition of individual inspiration becomes supremely important. I am quite satisfied that, however subconsciously, it is such a recognition that primarily supports us in the present war. We have an instinc-tive horror of being caught, regimented, dragooned by the Nazis. We want to keep clear of that at all hazard and cost, we

want to be forever free of it, and thus the only war aims we
have so far been able to formulate are contained in the one
word, freedom. However much of this precious freedom we
have lost, however little we may have actually had of it, still,
hang it! we had and have a lot more than the Nazis, and we're
going through with this bloody business in order that we shall
have still more of it, more than ever before, in the future.

It may be argued that much of this is mere feeling or
emotion and that the facts of the business put the whole issue
in a different light. The very notion of freedom is itself a myth.
Man is governed by relentless necessity, just like the bee. He
owes all he is and has to society. And so on. Most of which is
perfectly true.

But it is not the whole truth, in the same way as the wireless
set is not the whole symphony. When we talk of what man
owes to society we are really thinking of mutual benefits. But
he owes to society something more than can be included in any
economic equation of labour and goods: he owes it, as a
supreme gift, his inspiration, for it is on this inspiration from
the individual that society lives and remains a dynamic force;
without that inspiration, society becomes static like the beehive. Take away Beethoven, Sibelius and the other masters,
and where are our symphonies?

Ah, but, reply the political revolutionary, the big business
man, the publicist, and the European dictator, we agree; we
are struggling for a form of society in which individual inspiration will be given its maximum opportunity.

Now this is just where we have to go very carefully and ask
ourselves, as we did in the beginning, whether their real
concern is with the individual or with the power of the herd in
manifesting a herd theory. Why should I, for instance, instead
of attending here to my proper business of making personal
observations on natural history, have started this discussion at
all, unless I had become self-conscious about the value of such
observations, unless I had asked myself: Is it worth while
going on? Please do not misunderstand. The point is not
whether the work is done well or ill; it is whether it is worth
doing at all. And I would hardly have ventured to raise the

issue had I not observed distinguished writers on natural history troubled in the same way. Every now and again they grow self-conscious, they become apologetic.

In short, we have all come under the influence of mass theory, mass endeavour, mass emotion. Normal people will say that oh! all this is due to the war. But it is demonstrably not all due to the war. It could be argued, more cogently than not, that war is a result rather than the cause of it, as in fact we do argue that the war sprang from the blind mass-discipline of a Nazified Germany.

This mass-worship has become so insidious that it creeps between a man and his vision of a flower. The individual is no longer of value except as a unit in the mass. The shortest way to a concentration camp is by the expression of individual inspiration.

This, as I have said, is to me the great modern heresy. If evil is an active principle, then it is here contained in its purest form – that is, in the form of being most subtly destructive of the integrity of the individual. And it is not merely to be encountered in the vast and tragically obvious holocaust of war. It is everywhere. There is more than a joke in the thought that we go to a picture-house to enjoy the real thrills of love. Before we get the full kick out of anything we must watch it being publicly exhibited. No doubt when we have become complete neuters, like the working bees, we may still get a thrill from erotic exhibitionism by way of ancestral memory.

In making a stand, it is always the present that is of value here, because it is the present that creates the future. To say that there will be plenty of time to think about Nature and literature and art and all that when the war is over is merely the obvious symptom of the heresy. There won't be any more time. There will be exactly the same, but with the inclination gone weaker from disuse.

Nature is everywhere; the earth under our feet, wind or sun or rain in our faces whether crossing a street or a field. Each time that a man consciously puts himself into relation with some such manifestation of our planet, even if for no longer than a passing second, he commits his act of calm defiance against the herd tyranny. We need not less of this relation, but more. And when a man looks at a bird or feels the wind on his face we should want him to tell us, if telling is his job, not only what he sees but also how it affects him, in calm or in pleasantness or in ecstasy, so that we may nod in understanding and go about our business, however grim, with greater heart.

# For Christopher's Cap

*Unpublished [1957], National Library of Scotland*

You talk of conversational powers and speculative stamina – I can assure you there was plenty of both in those early years of the literary movement, which Christopher carried on so valiantly. Wondering if I could fix some sort of date, I looked up my copy of his *Contemporary Scottish Studies*, and beneath his signature on the fly leaf, he wrote: 'Inverness, 3rd January, 1927, 5.20 a.m.' Not a redundant word: precise, lucid and sober. So that night he must have been staying with me in the Highland capital. Probably there was a good-going foray on. I suspect it had something to do with what we called the Gaelic aristocratic idea, which we were then hunting with all the ardent zeal our ancestors devoted to lifting cattle. Accordingly that Grieve should assume the name of MacDiarmid [sic] seemed perfectly natural. That he in particular used the name MacDiarmid [sic] when writing in Lallans was merely an instance of that higher logic which embraced all Scotland, and was then prepared to use all Scotland as a starting point for a good-going cattle raid into England, and after that it was the wide, wide world. By five in the morning all this was wonderfully clear. However, my *particular* pleasure in it was the spirit of adventure. It was not just talk, not merely an indulgence in theories, literary or metaphysical or what you will. A real hunt was on. Should a few English literary cattle of doubtful pedigree show up in the offing, Christopher's nostrils would quiver in an inspiring way. Anyhow, I have the memory of exhilaration and occasionally a rare delight. And personally I have never found true delight present but the creative spirit was there also – and how richly Christopher has proved that now! So, when Edinburgh University sticks its eagle's feather in his bonnet, never in my view will it have stuck one in more appropriately.

# Is There a Living Scottish Tradition in Writing Today?

*'Scottish Life and Letters' BBC, 1959*

That simple scene of a boy gathering mussels for bait was followed by the boats going to sea with their baited lines. They were caught in a terrific winter storm and had to fight their way back against all the odds. The crews survived. Now the story was founded on fact. And I can still remember my astonishment – though it's nearly thirty years ago now – when a highbrow London magazine, criticising the book, said it fell short in its storm scene because it avoided tragedy. Yet to us, on the spot, the sheer wonder, the marvel, lay in the seamanship that so ordered the terrible fight in its final moments that death was given the slip with barely an inch to spare. Scenes like it were common enough all round our coasts – including the Islands, of course. That was what happened; that was the *tradition* in seamanship; and that was what I was paying tribute to.

Of course many changes have taken place in deep-sea fishing since the early years of this century when small open boats fought it out with sail. Boats got engines. The drudgery of baiting thousands of hooks was superseded by seine nets. Steam drifters went after the herring. The changes have been, no doubt, revolutionary. But through them all there has been no change in one thing: the tradition of seamanship. Whatever the material or mechanical changes, the human spirit, bred in that unchanging environment of cliff and storm, meets the sea's challenge with the same courage and inherited skill. The tradition continues.

For tradition goes very deep. Its essence, its spirit, changes little, if at all, over long periods of time. Recently I heard the rhythm of Hebridean seas in a Gaelic song on the wireless. Tradition has the song going back to the time of St. Columba. As I listened I got the feel of oars in my hands, and the swing of the sea under my dinghy, as I headed once more for a certain sandy beach on Iona. Then, in an instant, the oars were in the hands of monks, pulling for the same island, to the same sea's rhythm, the same tune, over thirteen centuries ago.

How, then, does it come about that we question the existence of a tradition and ask ourselves if it is still alive? Because his tradition is so natural to a man that it has become, as we say, second nature. It is the machinery, the instrument, through which his deepest nature expresses itself, and expresses itself so naturally that he is unaware of it. In fact occasionally he actually needs someone from outside to show it to him.

If I found myself, therefore, particularly interested in a recently published book called *The Scottish Tradition in Literature*, it was because it was written by a German, Kurt Wittig, a literary scholar of distinction and fine insight. Now this outsider not only found that a Scottish tradition in world literature existed, but he also isolated its fundamental and unique characteristics, in writer after writer, from the time of Barbour, from the battle of Bannockburn, right up until the present day. We may argue about his assessments of individual writers, but not about the literary tradition these writers have created and enriched throughout the centuries. This foreigner makes it quite plain. The Scottish tradition continues.

Perhaps, then, we question ourselves about a living tradition because the expression of it in writing and the arts is so utterly unpredictable. For example, as a youth, brought up within sight of the Orkneys and knowing something about them, could I have predicted that these islands, remote from city civilisations, would produce in my time Edwin Muir, Eric Linklater and Stanley Cursiter? So, for these Hebridean islands and their old Gaelic songs – the realist question surely is *not will* they, but *when* will they, produce their Sibelius?

But perhaps the nagging doubt has something to do with

size. In all this, is Scotland big enough to matter? Has size in our day become critically important? Well, let us try to check this by shifting our glance to a neighbouring country of about equal size and with similar Gaelic roots in an ancient past. Ireland. I know Ireland well, over many years, so let me name three Irish writers in my time: W. B. Yeats, James Joyce and Bernard Shaw. Next, let us go over the great nations of the world, from America and Russia to France and England, and try to find, in any one of them, in our time, three writers whose combined achievement in literature would compare with that of these three Irishmen. Who would quarrel with me if I concluded that Ireland topped the lot?

Ah, but, it may be objected, James Joyce, at least, was a superb innovator, a revolutionary, a world figure: what has he got to do with the Irish tradition? My reply must be brief and may therefore seem crude, but here it is: subtract Dublin from James Joyce and just how much is left?

No, luckily for us, we cannot get away from tradition. For tradition is the environment in which the creative spirit is at home to itself.

*Short Stories*

# The Dead Seaman

*Scots Magazine, 1931*

He turned his red-bearded face over his shoulder and looked at the weather coming in over the horizon. From beneath the cliffs on which he walked, the sea flattened and outreached coldly. Every now and then a burst of wind turned back on itself, much as the man's head turned back crouched and sniffing the weather. It was going to be a dirty night. The black and white collie, lean and sharp in intelligence as its fangs, kept close to heel.

There was still an hour's walk to the crofting township of Clachuain. By the time he got his provisions and looked in at Smeorach's the night would not be far off. They went on steadily. When he glanced over his shoulder again he saw the sea's teeth already whitening in the night's mouth. The brow of the horizon had lowered. A spit of rain was quicker than his eyelid. Not a likely night to carry home dry provisions! On the last upward roll of the moor he stopped and turned full round. The dog turned with him and together they surveyed the vast stretch of sheep moor, picking out signs and meanings that an untrained eye would have missed.

Indeed the normal eye would have caught nothing suggesting life unless it were the far roof of a small cottage set back a little from the cliffs; not that it would have caught even that were it not for the smoke, for the grey curved thatch was set in colour and shape to the earth. But when the man's eye rested on the smoke, he knew his brother was putting fresh peat on the fire. Because they lived alone, and observed rather than spoke, he saw his brother setting the peat on edge. His brother

would be making a good fire of it, you could be sure, now that
he was alone!

For a moment and vaguely this separate existence that was
his brother affected Dughall Ruadh like a dark underswirl of
water with a gleam in it. When a man was alone he could
stretch his body and let any sort of secret thought to his face
and be at his ease.

Dughall Ruadh continued on his journey, thinking all at
once that he would get back when he would get back, and time
enough. Seven miles each way was a fair step. He was forty-
five years old and was made uncomfortable by human beings
and had little to say. The craving to be amongst human bodies
therefore came upon him strongly at times. In Smeorach's he
would gratify his desire till the moon rose.

But by the time the moon rose the storm was at its height.
Smeorach himself seemed to be acted upon by the storm. His
voice when it rose out of the story's thickness caught a
whistling note, which probably explained his nickname of the
Smeorach or Mavis. Though he was nearly eighty years of age,
his eyes could grow bright as a bird's, when his eyelids
winking quickly made them twinkle.

Dughall Ruadh sat at one side of the fire, his large frame
hunched on a small chair, his low-set head, with its suggestion
of strength, set lower than ever, so that the eyebrows only at
odd times revealed gleams of eyes. Against his solid embodi-
ment the actions of the men and boys of the township were
sensitive and almost nervous. They listened attentively, but
always with the air of waiting for the moment to break away
and laugh (throwing a look at Dughall Ruadh).

When an elderly man came in he spoke directly to the
stranger, enquiring after his health, and his brother's health,
and the health of the sheep. Dughall replied shortly but
agreeably enough, then never spoke until he was again addressed.

The boys who, against parental instruction, slipped into the
ceilidh-house on the way home with their milk-pails, regarded
Dughall Ruadh with stealthy eyes. To them he was a figure of
heather and red sandstone taken out of a landscape or a

dream; yet familiarly mentioned in their school play with a certain laugh. 'I am Dughall Ruadh MacIain,' a boy would say with an outflung hand, as though he meant, 'I am Cuchullain.' Or again, 'I am Dughall Ruadh, the Bad Man' (which is to say, the Devil) and the boy's mouth would gobble up.

Even Smeorach was sensitive to Dughall's presence to such an extent that he rarely told his story to his face, but always with his shoulder to him addressing the others; yet when sometimes Dughall grunted as a good point was made, Smeorach quickened, his voice whistled, and he turned to Dughall Ruadh repeating the last sentence with happy triumph.

Under the influence of the storm the atmosphere within the old house grew lively and tense. It was the perfect time for recalling stories of storms and wrecks and dead bodies washed up by the ocean, of lonely old women living in cottages by the tide, of foreign sailors, of theft, and of voices in the night.

For this knuckle of the mainland had no lighthouse and the western sea brought many a tragic clue to its rocks and, at least once in a generation, tragedy itself. After a great storm boys would search the little bays for glittering keepsakes, while men bent double on a rope would haul at wooden wreckage.

Thus the storm excited them now in an eerie way and Smeorach moved them readily with the tale which his father had told him, and which they all knew in its midnight horrible detail, with its dark man who spoke in a tongue his father did not understand – the lifted face, the awful entreaty, and death, no one ever knowing who or what he was.

When Dughall Ruadh grunted at its climax, however, Smeorach instantly felt the comment was ironic, and, amazed and insulted, flashed at Dughall a glance.

'But I tell you it's the God's truth,' he whistled. 'Didn't it happen to my own father himself and didn't he tell me out of his own mouth?'

The others felt their skin grow cold as they watched Dughall, who got slowly to his feet.

'Who said I was doubting you? I was merely thinking it was

time I was off home.' A twist came to his face and his mouth
opened as if to yawn. In the silence Smeorach's eye began to
glitter.

'Is it mad you are that you would think of going home on a
night like this?' he demanded. The comment in his voice was
ironic, so that immediately he was more than even with
Dughall.

But Dughall muttered, 'It's not that much of a storm,' and
looked behind him for the sack in which he had put all his
provisions.

'And how will you find your way home on a night like this?
Do you think you'll see the moon and the rushing sky black as
the Earl of Hell's riding boots?' Smeorach enquired.

'I'm not a woman,' said Dughall, 'that I should need the
moon,' and laughed in an awkward, big way, 'taking off'
Smeorach. This was such an unusual effort on his part that no
one remembered to laugh with him.

'Very well,' blinked Smeorach. 'And if you feel tired on the
way you can put your head under the sack, for the rain will
have masked the tea and melted the sugar and turned the food
to brochan. You should fare well.'

Dughall Ruadh looked at his sack.

'Out of this house you will not go this night,' added
Smeorach. 'And that's that.'

And out of it he did not go, for the provisions were partly
his brother's, and costly. As the community's shepherds they
did little more than share one man's wages between them.

With the first of the daylight, however, he was up and
putting on his boots. Smeorach being an old man and a light
sleeper heard him. 'It sounds a calm morning,' he said. 'We
won't be seeing you again for a few weeks.'

'It's calm enough,' muttered Dughall. 'You won't see me
again for a time, that's true.'

Then he went away, Smeorach thinking in his heart that the
man was coarse, with no grace in him anywhere.

But in the forenoon, Smeorach, who was out taking the
bright air by the front door, saw a man and dog coming from
the cliffs. 'Here!' he cried to the policeman who was passing

and had not yet put on his uniform, 'that's not Dughall Ruadh coming there?'

The policeman turned to the moor. 'It looks like it,' he said.

'I wonder what on earth he can have forgotten that would have taken him all this way back at once?' Smeorach took a neighbourly step or two towards the policeman. By the time Dughall would have got home again he would have walked over twenty miles in a morning.

They waited together in silence until Dughall came up. Smeorach was going to have cried something at Dughall, but his long sight was good and he saw Dughall's face.

'Can I have a word with you?' said Dughall to the policeman; and they both walked away from Smeorach, of whom Dughall had taken no notice.

They came to a halt a little distance from the houses and stood talking together so earnestly that soon the whole township was secretly watching them.

At last they parted and Dughall turned on his heel and started back the seven miles he had come.

At once it was clear that something dreadful had happened. The policeman hung on his feet a moment, wondering what he should do first, then he went along slowly to the post office, where in time he composed a telegram of twelve words.

It reported a foreign vessel lost, one dead body at Sgeir, and was addressed to the Procurator-Fiscal. Then the policeman went home to consult with his wife and dress himself. He went about things slowly and with a thoughtful expression. But by good fortune a reply came in record time instructing him to get a doctor for examination of the body and giving a time for the Procurator-Fiscal's own arrival. 'Wasn't it lucky I hung on?' said the policeman to his wife. He had never had a case like this and his position was now clear. He went with a buttoned air to the post office and sent off a telegram to the doctor, who lived four miles away at Craignish. Then feeling his breast pocket again he set off by the cliffs to Sgeir.

Dughall Ruadh must have been watching for him for he came round the corner of the thatched house that he and his brother occupied while the policeman was still some distance away. He leaned against the wall, his head sunk so low in his shoulders that he appeared to stoop under a secret burden. The strangeness of this remote dwelling came upon the policeman as he drew near. With no woman about the place, what a queer life these two men must lead, seeing no living soul but themselves from one week's end to another! After greeting him the policeman asked: 'Where's your brother?'

'He's inside,' said Dughall, 'with the body.'

As they entered the living-room the policeman peered hither and thither through a yellow gloom of the dead that startled him. The air too was heavily tainted. His eyes fastened on a figure that rose slowly from the fire. Tearlach was fair rather than red like his brother Dughall, and now his shaven face was white and his eyes as they turned to face the policeman glistened noticeably. His features were finer and more mobile than his brother's, and he smiled as he stood in an odd attitude of expectancy.

The policeman turned his look to the small window, across which was a piece of brown sacking, then he faced into the room and on the bed in the inner corner he discerned the body.

He asked Dughall to take the sacking from the window, and when the light flowed in he went over and removed a cloth from the face, putting the flat of his hand at the same moment on the forehead. The hand drew back quickly, surprised by the cold, and the policeman, who was still in his thirties, began to stare at the face.

It was a face with distinct cheek bones and a fair pointed beard. It had an air of nobility and the discoloration of the skin gave it an extra strength in death. The bedclothes were drawn close up under the chin so that the face was cut off. There was a furrowing of the brows above the closed eyes that added to the nobility of the face a characteristic intolerance, almost the suspicion of a fierce anger. The policeman gently removed the bedclothes a little off one shoulder and saw that the body was naked. Then he replaced the clothes and turned from the bed. As he did so, Tearlach's eyes shifted from him to the window, through which they stared far to sea.

They were silent for a little, then the policeman said it was a great tragedy. The dead man's face affected him so much that he forgot for the moment his very natural concern to report the case properly, omitting no important detail. Presently, however, he took his notebook from his breast pocket and turned to Tearlach.

'You'll have to tell me,' he said, 'how it all happened from the beginning.'

'I'll do my best,' Tearlach replied. He found the policeman a seat near the window and a box on which he could place his notebook, for he had a ready movement that his brother lacked.

'You can sit down,' said the policeman to Tearlach.

So Tearlach sat down on one side of him and Dughall on the other, and as Tearlach went on speaking Dughall had difficulty in keeping his eyes off him.

'When did you have the first intimation of it?' asked the policeman.

'I was sitting here by the fire,' replied Tearlach, 'and I saw a glare coming behind me from the window.'

'What sort of a glare?' and the policeman turned and looked out of the window himself. Beyond the ridge of the cliff-tops was a series of low rocks in the sea running out from a headland. Tearlach watched the policeman pick up the rocks, then removed his eyes and said:

'At first I thought it was lightning, for the storm was blowing hard, but when I got up to the window and looked out I saw that it was flares from a ship.'

'What did you do then?'

'I went down to the shore as quick as I could. I had been down in the first of the night hauling up our own boat and making sure of her. At that time there was no vessel anywhere to be seen.'

'Now what did you observe when you went down?'

'I saw that a vessel was on the rocks there off the head and that nothing could save her. Although the moon was not out, there was a moon in it, so that it was not so dark but that I could see a little when my eyes got used to it. I heard cries. They came through the noise of the storm. I felt from the high sound of them that the vessel was going down.'

To translate the Gaelic, in which it was easier for both of them to speak, into good English took the policeman a little time, so that when Tearlach had finished answering a question there followed a silence through which the policeman's pencil wrote like fate's finger.

'You did not actually see the vessel herself?'

'I saw a bit of her side in a flare of red once, and then I could sort of see her black like a rock against the sea.'

'The sea was very stormy?'

'It was.'

'Yes. And what happened then?'

'I could do nothing else. I was shouting at the top of my voice when all at once I made out a strange shape on the water's surface coming swimming towards me. I got a start, but it was a man hanging on to his seaman's chest. I hauled him and the chest out of the water. But at that he never made a sound; he just fell over.'

'He just suddenly became unconscious?'

'He just lost all his senses.'

'But he was alive?'

'Yes.'

'How did you know?'

'I carried him up to the house here on my back and tried to waken him up, but I could not, so I took off his wet clothes and put him to bed to get him warm. The breath seemed to have gone out of him, but I felt his heart move in him once.'

'And what did you do then?'

'I boiled the kettle and tried to put hot tea between his teeth. I warmed a blanket and wrapped it round him. After a little I saw that he had passed away.'

'What did you do then?'

'I thought I should go down to the shore and see if there were any other men. So I went down. I took a light with me from the fire there and shouted. But I found nothing, except his chest, which I had forgotten. I brought it back with me.'

While the policeman was writing that down, Dughall's eyes swerved from his brother's face and looked down at his hands, lips pressed together and skin gathering in small hard wrinkles about the lowered lids.

'So you brought it back with you,' repeated the policeman. 'I see.' Then he looked up into Tearlach's face, almost with surprise. 'So you have it here then?'

Tearlach got up.

'Yes,' he said. 'That's it.'

Dughall stood aside and the policeman looked at the chest against the wall. He caught it by a metal handle at one end and pulled it more into the light. Then he straightened himself and looked at Tearlach.

'Did you open it?'

'No,' said Tearlach, looking back at the policeman.

The policeman studied the chest with a thoughtful expression that closely attracted the brothers. Then he stooped and tried to lift the lid.

'It's locked!' he said.

'Yes,' muttered Tearlach.

'You could hardly have opened it if it was locked,' said the policeman, scratching his cheek with the pencil. 'It's tight shut and likely waterproof. Where's his clothes?'

'On the chair there.'

'The policeman went to the fire and started methodically going through the pockets. There were three coins, a knife, and part of a tobacco stick.

'That's odd,' said the policeman, 'but likely he would have forgotten the key in his hurry.'

He stood looking at the chest and wondering exactly what he should do with it. It would have to be broken open, but it might be as well to have the Procurator-Fiscal or at least the doctor with him when he took such a step. In any case, there was no hurry for that. He straightened himself.

'And did you do anything more?' he asked Tearlach.

'What could I do? I sat here until it was daylight and then I went down to the shore to see if I could find anything.'

'And did you?'

'There's some wreckage. Not much. The wind was blowing more downshore than straight in. After that I went along the top of the rocks looking for any signs. But I saw nothing. I was feeling tired after the whole night, and when Dughall came back he said he would go for you himself.'

The policeman presently drew a quick line in his notebook. 'That's very good and clear,' he nodded. 'It's as clear as can be and you must be very tired after such a night. You did well.'

Tearlach wet his lips and stretched himself a little and smiled. 'The night was so long that I would like to forget it.' He got to his feet restlessly.

'Are you too tired to come down to the shore with me for a minute?'

'I'll be glad to do anything to help you,' said Tearlach, almost briskly.

The policeman thanked him and added: 'When we come back you'll just take a lie down.' He was a dark, broad, kind man.

Dughall Ruadh led them to the door, where he filled his chest with air, saying in an intimate tone to the policeman: 'It was a sad business.' He led them down to the shore. In one place the descent was very steep.

'Did you carry him up this?' asked the policeman.

'I did,' said Tearlach.

The policeman showed his admiration of the feat. The brothers became friendly towards him. Dughall indeed became almost talkative as he showed the policeman their boat, the tiny creek, and taking him up on the ledge of a rock pointed out where the ship went down.

The policeman examined the wreckage. Dughall Ruadh regarded his brother.

'Go away home,' he said to him. 'You're looking grey. I'll take Mr Mathieson out in the boat and we'll see if we can find anything more at all.'

'Do you that,' said the policeman. 'The others will be questioning you soon, but that will be a lot of formalities, and if you answer them as you answered me there will be no difficulty for any of us.'

'All right,' Tearlach said. 'I'll be going.' And he turned, side-stepping for a moment like a drunk man, and left them.

'Your brother went through a lot last night,' said the policeman, looking after him.

'He did that,' said Dughall, looking at the policeman.


Two hours later as the doctor drew near on his pony, the policeman walked out from the corner of the house to meet him. The doctor dismounted and they stood talking together, while Dughall remained leaning against the house.

Presently they came towards Dughall, the doctor nodding and saying: 'I understand.' He had got the whole story and what had happened was now quite clear to him. He greeted Dughall with friendly consideration, hitched his pony, and went round to the door. He was a clear-witted, straight-forward man with a mind of his own and led the way naturally into the kitchen, where the first thing that he saw was a body stretched out stiff before the fire with grey face and closed eyes. He went towards it and half-stooped. Dughall and the policeman were suddenly unable to move. The doctor, getting down on one knee, put his palm on the forehead, whereat Tearlach wakened up quickly, giving the doctor such a start that he backed away with a noise in his throat. In an instant Tearlach was on his feet, showing his teeth, while his disordered hair gave the impression of standing on end.

The doctor stuttered: 'What's this?'

Then the wind went out of them a little and the policeman explained, pointing to the bed. The doctor gave a harsh grunt and went and stood over the dead man.

The face must have attracted him at once from the way he stared at it. He examined it very closely and turned down the bedclothes from the bare chest. He went over the surface of the whole figure then returned to the throat and face.

His back was to the three men, who stood clear of the small window. Professional rites completed, the doctor drew up the bedclothes and, stepping thoughtfully towards the fire, considered with himself for a moment; then looking at Tearlach asked:

'You say the body was alive when it came ashore?'

'Yes.'

'Uhm.' The doctor withdrew his eyes a moment and then flashing them at Tearlach again asked: 'How long would it be from the time you carried him from the shore until he died?"

'It wasn't so very long.'

'How long – an hour, two hours?'

'I'm not sure,' Tearlach said, looking rather as if someone were still getting at him in his sleep.

'Think it out,' said the doctor. 'You carried him up here. What was the next thing you did?'

'I took off his wet clothes and put him to bed."

'And then?'

'I put on the kettle to make a cup of tea. I also warmed a blanket and put it round him.'

The doctor nodded 'Very good. And did he manage to take any of the tea?'

'He wouldn't open his mouth.'

'Did he open his eyes?'

'No.'

'How did you know he was alive?'

'I felt sure he was alive. I felt his heart, too, and it moved.'

'The doctor was thoughtful for a few seconds. 'He certainly got a bad bruising,' he said. 'It must have been the chest that kept him afloat. Let me see it.' He examined the chest. Then he got Tearlach to explain how the body clung to it.

The doctor remained gazing at the chest meditatively. 'Tell me,' he said suddenly, 'how long it was before he died after you tried to give him the tea?'

'Not long.'

'An hour?'

'Hardly, I should say.'

'What time of night would it be?'

'I never took the time, but it must have been getting on for the middle of the night.'

The doctor nodded slowly. 'That means he is dead for about fifteen hours. Yes, that should be pretty near it.' He seemed to be about to ask some further questions, but hesitated. Then he said to the brothers: 'Would you leave us for a little as we must consider our official report?'

The brothers withdrew and closed the door. After listening to their footsteps the doctor turned to the policeman and said: 'In my opinion, this is a case of strangulation.'

The policeman regarded the doctor with great astonishment.

'Come here,' said the doctor, and he proceeded to show to the policeman encircling marks on the neck and the congested colouring of the face. He turned down the bedclothes. 'Of course, there are bruises all over. He must have had a terrible time with wreckage or rocks or something. But these marks' – and he pointed to the neck –'are in my opinion the result of pressure – how applied, of course, I cannot say.'

'You think that he was strangled with someone's hands?'

'Well,' said the doctor, 'who can say definitely?'

The policeman was silent and quite still. The doctor looked at him.

'This is not a charge, you understand. We had better say no more about it until the Fiscal comes. Certainly say nothing to them,' and he indicated the brothers.

'All right,' nodded the policeman, his excitement eased by a clear line of action.

The following afternoon the Procurator-Fiscal conducted his examination in the same place. The seaman's chest was forced open and inside were found ship's papers and clothes. From the papers it was apparent that a certain Swedish vessel had foundered and that her crew of thirteen had been lost. The dead man, who had nearly fought his way through, must have been the ship's master.

The next point that emerged was that the man on the bed must have certainly died long before Dughall returned from Clachuain round about, say, eight or nine o'clock in the morning. The doctor was satisfied that death had occurred about midnight or shortly thereafter.

The only living person therefore with any direct personal contact in the case was Tearlach MacIain.

The three of them sitting like a tribunal called Tearlach before them. The Procurator-Fiscal questioned him closely,

but his answers were substantially those he had already given
to the policeman. To begin with he was more at ease than on
the previous day, though there was still something flashing
and uncertain, a little wild, in an occasional aspect. This was
understandable in one who lived for the most part a solitary
life, and who could not help feeling that he had come before
men who were questioning him very particularly. Once indeed
he flushed, but quickly became pale and reasonable again.

'Let me see,' said the Procurator-Fiscal, with a reflective
bearing on the evidence. 'The body came swimming in with
the chest. How did you catch it?'

Tearlach hesitated.

'Let me be the body,' suggested the Fiscal, 'and the table
here the chest. You follow me? You are on the shore there.
Now – catch me.'

After a moment Tearlach caught the Fiscal's head, the
fingers naturally passing under the ears and against the throat.

'Do you see that, doctor?' cried the Fiscal.

'Yes,' answered the doctor.

As the Fiscal came erect again he added: 'And there would
be the whole weight of the body to haul.'

Tearlach looked as if he were accused of having done
something wrong. 'I only caught him like that for a moment,'
he said, 'until I was able to reach farther down.'

'Quite so, quite so,' nodded the Fiscal agreeably. Then he
turned to the question again of whether or not the body was
really alive in the house. But now Tearlach was growing
dogged. A veil, faintly mistrustful or hostile, came over his
face.

'Anyway, you could not say you saw him die at any
particular moment?'

'No.'

'You just suddenly realised he was dead?'

'Yes.'

There was silence for a moment.

'All right. Thank you.'

When he had gone the Procurator-Fiscal said : 'He is
beginning to get a bit distressed and, I think, a little suspicious

of us. The point is that the seaman may have been dead here all the time, but he will never now admit it; I mean, he will never admit that he may have been mistaken. Once you have said a thing you've got to stick to it, for the law is a holy terror!' He smiled drily. 'However, what has happened is, I think, fairly clear now. In the first place I think you will agree with me that in a body so bruised it would be difficult to maintain the supposition that it was strangled.'

'On the contrary,' said the doctor, 'that is my only point ; it was strangled. How or why, of course, I don't know.'

'Quite. What I really meant was that these marks on the neck like some of those on the body might have been inflicted in various ways. For example, the neck might have been caught amongst wreckage, just as we are satisfied the leg was where the bruise goes almost right round. If that had happened he would have been about all in when he reached the shore. And Tearlach's helping hands would – you know – have possibly finished the job.'

'Possibly,' said the doctor. 'Only Tearlach insists the man was alive here for some considerable time after he had been carried from the sea. That hardly points to strangulation in the sea.'

Not if he *was* alive – which, as you can see from the evidence, is anything but clear. I think if I were to put it to you that the sailor *was* dead before he reached this cottage, you would agree with me?'

'I would.' And the doctor smiled.

'Quite,' nodded the Procurator-Fiscal. Then he went on: 'There is no doubt that this man Tearlach has a clear consistent image of what happened. He did his best to save and revive a man and naturally expects some credit for it. Let us, however, consider the opposite – that is, that he was strangled by human hands on shore ; that is, presumably, by the man who brought him here. In view of the facts and the complete lack of evidence or of any witness the charge would be monstrous. There is, moreover, a complete lack of motive. Why do it? And if for any inconceivable motive he did want to do it, why bring the body here? Or, having brought the body here first, why not then dispose of it very simply by throwing it over the rocks? There was no one here to see; no one ever to know. And the man is palpably not a fool, not abnormal or in any way deranged. Why does he even say the body was living – keeps on insisting it was living – when it would be so simple and convenient to say it was dead – or at least that he was uncertain? There could not even be a personal motive, for the seaman is a stranger, a foreigner.'

'I quite agree,' said the doctor. 'It would be fantastic to accuse this man. I certainly would never make any suggestion of that sort.'

'If there was even the very slightest doubt or suspicion it would be my duty to present the case accordingly, and I should most certainly. But there is not only none ; there is on the contrary the fact that this man carried the seaman up that steep place and tended him and tried to bring him back to life. He then hunted the shore and generally speaking did his utmost. No sane person but would have praise for him. And it is not part of my duty to bring unsupported suspicion against any subject who has acted in a way that is not merely innocent but definitely praiseworthy. I think that is about the true position. I shall make all the usual inquiries about these people and report accordingly.'

And so it came about that death by misadventure was agreed, and the foreign sailor was buried in a corner of the local churchyard, the minister having sanctified the occasion by a powerful and moving prayer on the subject of those who go down to the sea in ships.


In the crofting district and township of Clachuain the sheep farm was a new experiment in communal effort, and one that was watched by every individual, whether personally involved or not, with close concern. Dughall and Tearlach could by original agreement have had a share in the profits if they had also contributed their share of the stock. Like many others and for the same reason, this they had been unable to do, although in every case the opportunity, greatly coveted, was still open upon certain terms.

The lives of the two shepherds were naturally a source of much talk to the people of that country, for they were good shepherds and lived the lonely life around which reflection in its more curious forms tends to gather. Always the women of Clachuain wondered how these two big men lived 'out yonder,' while it was said that when one or other drove to a sale there was a rough night or two before the journey back. Strong men of coarse fibre guided by dogs of such cunning and intelligence as made schoolboy fables.

Now early one morning, about a month after the death of the foreign seaman, Dughall Ruadh, driving home twelve sheep, was overtaken by a crofter who was on his way to try the line fishing at sea.

'Hurro, Dughall,' said the crofter, 'have you been buying sheep for yourself?'

Dughall answered, 'Yes.'

The crofter laughed.

Dughall turned his look upon him. 'Isn't it time I was able to buy a few sheep?'

After an acute glance the crofter hid himself within his astonishment, remarking how lucky Dughall was and how glad he was that Dughall was lucky.

Dughall's expression was harsh as though he had had a heavy night. The red hairs stuck out on his face. He said that truly he was lucky to buy anything considering all he got.

'None of us make so much that we can buy sheep every day,' said the crofter good-humouredly.

'You have your share whatever,' said Dughall. And the tone of his voice added: 'So what the devil's right have you to talk anyway?'

Now though the crofter was annoyed with Dughall he was far more amazed. When in a few minutes he joined his friends by the fishing-boat his face exhibited amusement.

'I met Dughall Ruadh going home there with some sheep. He must have had the wild night!'

'Going home with sheep – at this hour!'

They laughed with understanding wonder.

'Yes, and when I said to him that I was glad to see he had been buying some sheep for himself, he wanted to know why the devil he wouldn't be buying sheep for himself.'

'That was one for you!'

'Yes, I was taken aback. I didn't think he had a penny to buy sheep.'

'Do you mean the sheep *were* his?'

'Yes,' said the newcomer with a cunning simplicity.

They all regarded his smiling face.

So that by the afternoon everyone in Clachuain knew that Dughall Ruadh had driven home his own sheep.

There was no reason at all why Dughall should not have driven home his own sheep. That was the oddest thing of all.

'It just shows you,' remarked a friendly man to Smeorach, 'how it is possible for those who live carefully to save up their money.'

'It shows all that,' said Smeorach, 'fully.'

Smeorach's mind seemed to get hung up listening to words at once cunning and apocalyptic. Then he looked at the man – who was looking straight before him.

When two boys dropped into the ceilidh-house that night with their milk-pails they were aware of a pause in the talk, and of everyone looking round at them almost as though they were expecting something or anything. Yet the talk went on again, each man starting a new subject with difficulty. Smeorach was all politeness and the telling of a story was not even thought about.

Yet when the boys left that house in the darkness they were more frightened than usual and stuck together, throwing glances behind them every other step. For the thing that haunted them now was a dead body with a bruised ring round the throat where it had been strangled.

Even in Smeorach's, however, no mention had been made of *that*. Once a man dropping in from an outlying croft had said with a smile: 'I hear Dughall Ruadh is buying sheep.'

'So we hear,' Smeorach agreed, also with a smile. Then everyone waited, smiling and looking at the fire, listening to the silent monstrous joke until the man said: 'Well, he's lucky.

I wish I could afford to buy a few,' and stretched himself negligently.

'You've a good bit of ground west yonder.'

'I have,' said the man. 'In fact, as you might say, I have everything but the money.'

'Ah, the money!' said Smeorach.

'It's the devil an' all, the money!' said another.

'I wouldn't mind coming on a box of it myself,' said a humorous man, and he turned playfully and caught one of the boys by the shoulder asking: 'What do you say, Iain? Eh? How's your mother to-night?'

'She's better,' said the boy shyly.

Then they all turned to the fire again, the subject of money exerting over all others a fatal attraction, so that they could not get quite away from it and from its hidden humour.

A second month passed by and then early on a Sunday morning the minister of Clachuain, who had been called out to visit an old woman whose time had come, happened full upon Dughall Ruadh driving home sheep before him.

For a moment the minister was overcome and stood gazing on this unholy work, this breaking of the Sabbath, as upon an activity wholly of the devil. Then his wrath quickly moving in him, he overtook Dughall.

'What's this you're doing on the Lord's Day?' he demanded.

Dughall Ruadh did not look at him. His dog slid quietly to heel. But the minister had been praying a little while before and instructing God how to receive into His hands the spirit of their sister, and the greatness of this was upon him.

'Do you know,' he cried, 'what God's judgment will mean to you?'

Dughall Ruadh paid no heed to him, his face red and obstinate, his clothes creased and stained as though he had not shed them for a week.

'Dughall MacIain,' said the minister, 'have you no fear of God's wrath that you should drive home sheep as if His Sabbath was a market day?'

'I'll drive home sheep any day, *if I like*,' said Dughall

Ruadh, and lifting a hand that almost hit the minister's face sent the collie to turn the sheep off the road.

The minister watched that flock and its damned shepherd move on to the moor, then resumed his homeward journey, his head bent in a fierce concentration.

The people knew of this as they filed into church; they knew of it from the text; they knew of it from the awful restraint of the manner. It was the hour for evildoers to flee from the wrath to come.

Over the minds of the worshippers the sermon had from the first a dark and dreadful power. Light flashed in it and the terror of omnipotence. The power grew, the terror marched, until the very House of God heard the evildoer named. 'Dughall MacIain,' thundered the voice now, under the up-lifted hand, 'may drive home sheep on the Sabbath *if he likes,* but I am here to tell Dughall MacIain that God will throw him into the burning pit of Hell – *if he likes.*' And the fist fell.

Little Iain's flesh went shivering cold as the eternal punishment of a burning Hell rose up before him. For little Iain knew what the minister did not yet know, namely, that Dughall Ruadh had been driving home *his own sheep.*

It was the custom for people to remain within their own doors on the Sabbath. On the afternoon of the sermon of denunciation an old woman saw a neighbour's dog slink through the lonely world beyond her window and she shook her head saying: 'I wonder at them.'

On the Monday the world was peopled again and by Wednesday night certain reckless spirits were dropping into Smeorach's, hungry for a secret laugh.

And because the laugh had to be in secret it tended to grow ribald, and one man asked broadly: 'I wonder how the devil Dughall Ruadh got the money?'

'The devil knows. He certainly got it somewhere.'

'Yes, in a lump.'

'A lump in your chest!'

'Whose chest?'

'Be quiet, my heroes,' said Smeorach. 'And, anyway, that chest was locked.'

They all smiled knowingly and with a fine excitement.

'It's an easy thing to lock the door when the beast is gone.'

No man made a direct statement, yet within an hour there was created a clear picture. It was this: Dughall's brother, Tearlach, had carried the seaman and his chest up to the house. In the seaman's wet clothes, which Tearlach took off him, had been the key. With the key Tearlach had opened the chest while the seaman was still half dead. Within the chest he had found money. The seaman began to recover. But it wouldn't do for the seaman to recover now. So he didn't recover. And the chest had been locked and the key thrown away.

Hadn't the doctor been sure of what he had been sure?

'Look you,' said Smeorach, for the daring talk was enough to chill the marrow, 'it might be – we may go as far as saying that – it *might* be that Tearlach came on a little boxie thrown up by the sea and belonging to no one. I'm judging no man's actions, but what we have found on the seashore we have often kept ourselves. That may be the sensible way of it. But, mind you, I'll say this myself that I think that Dughall bought the sheep with money that himself and his brother will have been saving up for years upon years like any other Christian man.'

'Certainly the Sabbath was the great day for Dughall the Christian to drive home sheep. At least according to the minister!'

'Supposing,' said Smeorach, in answer to this shot, 'that you had done something. And supposing, moreover, that the evidence of what you had done was there to be seen. And supposing, furthermore, that you could drop that evidence into a black night of storm so that it would be swallowed up for ever. Supposing all that, for the fun of it?' said Smeorach.

'*Dhè*, I don't know!' said the man with a shudder of a laugh.

'But supposing,' said another man with such a quiet tone that they all looked at him, 'supposing – that you did not know the evidence would be there?'

They all saw discoloration coming so slowly to a throat that the one who caused it would never think of it, would never see it with the throat covered.

This made them restless and for a little no man could gather his wits. There was something unlawful in the picture – and full of light. A picture not to look on, no, God shield us, when all is said.

'You can suppose anything,' said Smeorach.

'So I suppose,' said the quiet man.

Smeorach got up and put a peat against the fire. 'Do you think that yourself?' he asked.

'We weren't thinking,' said the quiet man, 'we were supposing. And as you say one can suppose anything. But what did you think I was thinking?'

Smeorach half turned and looked at the man.

At that moment the outer door opened, footsteps came to the inner door, and a figure with a sack on its back stood in the gloom of the entrance.

They all stared and Dughall Ruadh's eyes, shifting from one to the other, gleamed. Behind him his dog's eyes gleamed steadily.

'God bless us, is it yourself, Dughall? Come in! Come in!' cried Smeorach suddenly in a welcoming voice so high and eager that it whistled. The others moved quickly, making way, all of them lively and smiling before the advent of the stranger.

They were very hospitable to Dughall, who dropped his sack on the floor and took his chair in the corner.

'I'm not going to wait long.'

'Why all the hurry?' cried his host. 'It's a good night for walking and you come with the moon.'

'It's a good night enough.'

'Well then,' said Smeorach.

Dughall Ruadh said nothing.

'How are things with you?' asked the quiet man.

'They'll do,' said Dughall.

'So long as they're no worse,' and the quiet man spat in a friendly way in the fire.

'That reminds me,' interposed Smeorach hurriedly. He told his story with vivacity, his eyes twinkling like a bird's. Some threw in remarks and laughed and leaned back. Smeorach never had a more appreciative audience.

Soon Dughall Ruadh got up.

'You're not going already?' asked Smeorach amazed.

'What's all your hurry?' asked the quiet man quietly.

'I'll be going,' said Dughall Ruadh. As he hung a moment his face and his beard filled the room. Then he turned away, all crying good-night after him.

When Smeorach came back from seeing him beyond the door they glanced up at him.

'I'm sure I don't know,' said Smeorach, and went and sat down thoughtfully.

'What's to know?' asked the quiet man. 'Why wouldn't he come in as usual?'

'Why wouldn't he indeed?' acknowledged Smeorach with penetrating politeness.

Though their heads were now bent, their minds lifted to the man striding darkly across the moor, the sack on his back, and for a few moments the room was quite still.

As the months grew this stillness would inhabit the mind of any man thinking of the two shepherds alone in their house. As for the more daring boys, they would scout on to the moor on a Saturday to get a glimpse of Dughall Ruadh or Tearlach in the distance. Flat in the heather they would recount the most bloody deeds, until getting to their feet they would rush back in the broadest daylight, the devil himself at their heels, laughing and shouting when a little one left behind began to scream frenziedly, until one boy, more sensitive than the others, would turn back for the little one and slap it in his anger, screaming to it to shut up.

One night a year after the foreign ship had been wrecked, Dughall and his brother Tearlach were sitting in their cottage. In the light of a peat fire Dughall was whittling the head of a crook out of a lump of dried hazel. Tearlach, sitting farther back, was slightly in shadow and watched his brother in silence. The long soft flames flipped and threw shadows.

Presently Dughall began to make hissing noises in his teeth. His brows gathered as his head tilted to examine his rough workmanship.

Tearlach saw the brows and lowered his eyes. On his pale face a faint smile hovered and passed. His chin drooped to his chest, which was sunk inward as he lay hunched up. An extra flurry of wind shook the window.

'It's working up,' said Dughall, pausing for a moment.

Tearlach said nothing.

Dughall began to hiss more freely than ever in notes that searched for their melody as vaguely as the crook-head searched for its pattern. Yet each hiss was as distinct as the knife cut.

Dughall's red-whiskered face grew warm and blown a little. The brows lowered ever more readily. Tearlach's face gathered a sardonic expression as it slipped from Dughall's to the fire.

Dughall went on whittling. Once he opened his mouth and scratched the hair on a cheek noisily with his finger nails. The muscles of his mouth were taut. Suddenly he threw a concentrated look at his brother – whose eyes were dreamily on the fire. Dughall's chair scraped loudly.

The wind hit the window like the wings of a surprised bird. It cried going round the gable-end.

'It's worse it's getting,' said Dughall.

Tearlach, whose face had quickened at the wind-cry, now moistened his lips and replied: 'It sounds like it.' His voice seemed quite natural and again Dughall threw him a fierce and disappointed look.

All day Tearlach had been in one of his queer moods. And now Dughall felt he was sitting watching him and thinking odd thoughts. He did not like that. In fact, at any moment it might goad him to excessive anger. For what he was not quite sure of was yet a strange and disturbing knowledge.

He lost the melody altogether and hissed notes of no tune. Then he became aware of his hissing and stopped it. The wind shrieked. Dughall could no longer contain himself. He said in a loud voice to the room: 'I hope the boat's all right.'

Tearlach did not move.

'I say, I hope the boat's all right! ' cried Dughall thickly.

'Why wouldn't she be all right? ' Tearlach asked.

'You know the storm is coming in on a spring tide.'

Tearlach did not answer for a moment, then he said almost casually: 'She's as high up as usual.'

On the back of his words came an extra booming from the rocks, narrowing in a most unusual way into a shout. This shout broke into a final tumult.

Tearlach's lips had come apart. They closed and took moisture from the tongue.

'Well, that's not high enough on a night like this. Go down and see.' Dughall's voice was harsh and ill-tempered.

Tearlach did not move.

Dughall stopped whittling altogether. His red beard bristled. 'Will you go down and see?'

'Why should I?' asked Tearlach in a quiet, mocking tone.

'Because one of us will have to go,' shouted Dughall, 'and you have been doing nothing all the damn day!'

The younger brother got slowly to his feet with a weary smile. Then he recognised what he was doing and looked at his chair almost regretfully. His mouth twitched and he turned his face to the window. A far flash of lightning hit him in the eyes and he cowered back.

Dughall looked at him.

Tearlach was breathing quickly and his shoulders gave a hunch that was like a shudder. As he straightened himself his eyes flickered dangerously. Slowly he turned his back to his brother, hesitated a moment, then walked towards the door, his tawny collie at his heels.

Dughall found himself breathing quickly. He started whittling again in a mutter of relief.

Every now and again, however, he listened. The way his brother walked to the door, he might have made some terrible decision against the urge of his nature.

Dughall Ruadh began to feel uncomfortable and when suddenly there was the whine and scrape of a dog at the door, his skin crept.

For a little he tried to make himself believe he had heard nothing, then found himself being forced to the door, which he opened carefully.

At once Tearlach's dog slunk in, his tail between his legs, his belly almost on the ground, whining in the most unearthly manner.

'What is it?'

But the dog hid from him under the table.

At once Dughall got charged with energy. He shouted to the dog: 'Come here!' The dog, whining, crept a yard towards him. 'Curse you, come here!' yelled Dughall.

The dog crept back under the table.

'Damn you, you brute!' Dughall snatched a burning peat from the fire, and with a cry to his own dog strode from the house.

The rush of wind fanned the burning end of the peat to a glowing torch. Probably Tearlach had fallen in the dark and broken his leg, he said to himself in a loud inward voice. The loudness of the voice was to smother the knowledge that if Tearlach had fallen and broken his leg his dog would have led Dughall to him. The dog would have led Dughall if Tearlach had fallen and broken his neck.

In the middle of the steep descent Dughall shouted, 'Tearlach!' Again at the foot he paused and called to his brother in a savage voice. The fume of the sea was now on his face. The rock-thunder filled his head. The water came in long evil swirls to smash and spout. The force of all this was in Dughall's body. He was drunk with a fierce energy. Hands that clenched could murder a whole crew.

'Tearlach!' God damn him, where on earth had he gone! He came over against the boat. 'Tearlach!'

All at once his dog whined at his heels. Dughall jumped and then tried to kick the brute in the belly. Whining, the dog slid away. Dughall stooped and under the lee of the boat saw his brother's ghost-white face. It gibbered at him like the face of a monkey.

The peat dropped from Dughall's hand and he swung round snarling upon the darkness. In the darkness was the flicker of red eyes. Dughall saw black sea-bodies coming in upon him. He stooped and grabbed stones, his throat raking. He threw the stones in a frenzy of violence. The red peat-points faded, and left the slithering, treacherous darkness.

Dughall faced it, his chest rising and falling in fierce gulps, his nose snoring with his throat.

Facing it still, he stooped and caught his brother, heaved him up against himself, crushing the gibbering mouth and the writhing arms. The sea-arms swung sinuously and smashed and spouted. Dughall backed away with his brother, whose mouth never ceased to babble and whose body stirred to spasmodic jerks, in which, however, there was no force. It was as though in some dreadful moment Tearlach had put forth all his strength and been broken. There was left no trace at all of human speech in the animal sounds he made.

It would be difficult to say what might not have happened to Dughall Ruadh on that menacing shore had he not had his brother to protect. But the panic that comes from primal fear was held by a primal anger. He shouted at the darkness, he challenged it; with a half-formed horrible knowing, he shouted at the stealthy murderous forces, as if they were black figures of revenge come up out of the sea. His eyes leapt warily as he cursed and backed, crushing his brother to him.

The short, tense struggle of the steep ascent eased his mind and when he got his brother inside the cottage, he closed the door with a clash of triumph and bolted it.

Tearlach, released, went on into the kitchen, his shrunk body rustling inside its clothes. The face of one hand rubbed noisily the back of the other. From his mouth there came now a sound like the continuous moaning of a child through chittering teeth.

Dughall, intent on his own fight, swung to the window, which he shut out with a double fold of canvas sacking. Guarded at last he listened to the thunder of the storm in the rocks. His ears detected all manner of violent sounds and once a thin unnatural scream. This suddenly came nearer . . . was about the house.

A noisy gibbering behind made him swing round. Crouched

on his chair, Tearlach was opening and shutting a mouth of bared teeth in time to the opening and shutting of fierce claw-hands. It was a madman's picture of impotent ferocity.

Dughall stood staring at his brother, utterly unable to move.

For the first time that night the fear that is ugly and dissolves the flesh and makes slippery the tentacles of the mind came upon him. Wind-wings flattened against the window; the door rattled violently. With a wild oath Dughall staggered to mid-floor. He repeated the oath. He raised his voice against the demons of the night. He cursed the dead of the sea who came alive. In a great voice he dared and denied and damned. He feared nothing. He was Dughall MacIain. His red beard flared. Out of his dreadful terror he flung a mad defiance.

Breathing heavily and moving his neck, he swayed a moment, fists stuck out, then he went to his brother, who was now mumbling quietly to himself out of a hideous and unhuman smile.

He took off his brother's jacket and boots. 'Come on, you must go to bed … Be quiet,' he said to him. He handled him like a father handling a broken son. 'Hssh, be quiet, man! ' He lifted him into bed. 'Lie down there. No, no; lie down. Lie down, Tearlach, for God's sake!'

He got him down at last and, with a wary look at door and window, went to the fire. A good fire with plenty of leaping flames to brighten the place. He would get the old broken lamp out and try to light it. Put the kettle on and make some hot tea. Flames and light and heat.

A choking sound came from the bed.

Dughall swung round. His brother was clutching at his throat, eyes sticking out, mouth open and gasping.

The dreadful sight for a moment paralysed Dughall. Then he lunged at the bed and tore Tearlach's hands from his throat.

'What are you doing? God, what are you doing?'

Tearlach gibbered excitedly. If he had had any strength he would have been difficult to hold. He was gibbering straight in front of him, straining. All at once his head jerked to one side to gaze past Dughall.

At that, power went from Dughall and a sickness came into his throat. Sweat broke out on his forehead. With clenched teeth and breathing loudly through cold nostrils he slowly heaved round.

There was nothing there.

The sickness grew on him. He got off the bed. Cold waves swept his skin. His legs were trembling so that they had to take him quickly to the chair. His hand came up against his face, crushing the eyes and slipping upward against the wet brow. As he looked at the bed again he saw that the clothes were caught up under the chin as in the case of the dead sailor.

The storm pressed the cottage. The rocks boomed. The wind smashed and shook, whining in its eager lust to tear asunder. As, divided, it rushed on, its bafflement was a note of dying horror.

Dughall, holding to his chair, dragged his eyes from the place where the seaman's chest had been to door and window.

For Dughall had known only of the money which Tearlach said he had found amongst the seaman's belongings. What gear the sea throws up, the poor keep. That they should have given up what the sea placed in their hands would have been great folly.

No seaman would have come back out of the sea – *for that.*

Dughall got to his feet. He swayed a moment, listening. Then he went to the bed and stood by his brother. Looking down at him he now saw a faint darkness encircling the throat.

Slowly the blood of his body, the blood of brotherhood, warmed and spread its warmth over his body, in unspeakable intimacy, in profound understanding. Erect at the centre of this blood-loyalty, Dughall felt his confidence come breathing upward upon him, his strength, his courage. Than this blood-loyalty nothing was stronger. The forces of Hell could look out now. His brother's fingers began their restless dance. Dughall stilled them with a quiet hand.

'It's all right, Tearlach,' he said gently. 'It's all right. I'm here.'

Tearlach died a week later, having recovered neither his speech nor his reason.

The night of the burial there were many men in the ceilidh-house.

'The doctor laughed when he heard of the minister's prayer,' said the quiet man.

'Why did he laugh?' asked Smeorach.

'He laughed for two reasons. The first was that whatever anyone might say of Cain and Abel there was one thing certain of Dughall and Tearlach, and that was, according to the doctor, that Dughall *was* his brother's keeper.'

'What was there to laugh at in that?'

'I don't know,' said the quiet man.

As they all knew that this implied that those who preached brotherhood sometimes failed to practise it, themselves included, they were silent.

'And what was the other reason?' asked Smeorach.

'The other reason was that Tearlach would know that everyone thought he had strangled the seaman, whether he had done it or not.'

'And who started the idea of strangling at all I should like to know if it wasn't the doctor himself?'

'The doctor said,' continued the quiet man, 'that it was just possible that the poor devil – it's his own words – that the poor devil in his madness may have tried to strangle himself out of – out of having been made to think about it so often.'

This grew with the silence into a more terrifying thing in their minds than if the spirit of a murdered man had tried to strangle Tearlach.

'It's very queer then,' said one, 'that it should have happened exactly one year to the very night that the foreign seaman himself was strangled.'

'All the same,' said the quiet man, 'remember we don't know what happened that night to Tearlach on the shore. We don't know what he saw. No one will ever know.' He looked at Smeorach, 'What do you think he saw?'

'God save us!' said Smeorach.

'Amen,' said the quiet man.

# Birdsong at Evening

*Cornhill Magazine, 1926*

## I

As he drifted down the street to his lodgings, a queer lightness came to Mr Pope's feet, an uncertainty to his knees. His packing was finished. Had been for days. With an odd sense of unreality he moved about the somewhat disrupted diggings, barking his shins now and then on obtrusive angle of box or packing-case, discovering an overlooked razor-strop on the back of the bath-room door, approaching the window a score of times to see if his cab were coming.

An unreal evening altogether; so that it was not until the following morning that he finally realised he was cut adrift from – a lifetime.

The realisation came to him not unhappily. His watch by his bedside told him it was precisely twenty minutes to eight – as it had told him first thing in the morning for over forty years. Twenty minutes to eight – heave off the bedclothes – pivot out the legs.

Mr Pope lay still, eyes on the little window with its glowing yellow blind. He listened. A bird was singing on a tree down the little garden in front. A rumbling of cart wheels, a thudding earthy sound as of someone striking a potato-pit with the flat of a spade, the clatter of a bucket....

He took it all in, the strangeness of it – and lay still. He was not to get up for another hour. Nothing to call him now, to compel him to get up. He was his own master. Bedroom, sitting-room, all found – for twenty-five shillings a week. And his departmental pension ran to £125 p.a. Not to speak of the bank nest-egg. Wealth enough – and just as inexhaustible as himself.

Yet his legs twitched. He turned over to make himself more comfortable. Ah, splendid! ... But presently he yawned and looked at his watch again. Five to eight. Pity, after all, he hadn't set breakfast a little earlier. Such a fine morning! At eight – he pivoted.

He would take time over his shaving. He dawdled and hummed. Hum-um-um-ummm.... But he was still early on going downstairs.

'Couldn't resist such a fine morning, Mrs Gill,' he apologised timidly.

'Any hour as suits, Mr Pope,' replied the kindly woman, smiling with excellent good nature. 'I hope you had a good night?'

'Splendid! Like a top!'

'I'll get your breakfast in a jiffy. Heard you stirring.' And she bustled off.

He rubbed his hands, looking round upon his private den of a sitting-room. Hum-um-um-ummm....

Breakfast over, he strolled gently forth. He knew the place just well enough to find it at once familiar and strange. Down the little garden, noting the gold of crocus and green spears of sprouting other things, and so to the road. The road declined gently to the little town, but for him it was all country and a child's memory of a wooded stream.

He walked on. But as he walked he found himself curiously unable to collect his thought and concentrate it on the world around him. It came more easily to concentrate on – Tompsett pulling a ledger from the rack and posting up. He saw his rather bold writing, the decisive, curly way he finished off his 3s and 5s. Poor Tompsett! On such a spring morning! He took off his hat.

He fanned himself with his hat, though the air was cool enough. The exercise was unusual and his legs trembled a little. He sat down. From the belt of trees that wound with the river came a wonderful outpouring of birdsong. He listened and nodded. Delightful accompaniment to fresh air and freedom! Tompsett would be telling them that he, Pope, would be going to bits; no hobby. Poor Tompsett!

He returned from his walk a little tired and sought the comfort of an armchair. Even with its lack of springs it was grateful. Lunch would be in – let him see – one hour and a half! For a moment something like dismayed astonishment gripped him. Then his face cleared. Delightful, of course! In the afternoon he would go for a walk up the other side of the stream. Time – he had tons of it.… An hour or so later – 'I'm just fiddling about,' said Mr Pope aloud and unthinkingly. Then he paused in his aimless pacing and listened to the echo of the words in his mind. 'I'm just fiddling about,' said the echo, and looked rather queerly at Mr Pope.

## II

By the end of a fortnight Mr Pope knew both sides of that stream for a considerable distance pretty intimately. He also knew some other things, but so very intimately, those other things, that he could not as yet admit them to himself. It took one of these afternoons that occasionally invade the rigorous youth of spring with sultry languors, thunder-laden clouds and oppression, to draw a little of this self-knowledge from the secret places.

Hat in hand, the small figure shuffled on. Every now and then a handkerchief mopped at the beaded perspiration. The mouth had relaxed to permit an easier passage to breathing which had become a little noisy.

Suddenly a dizziness obscured his sight, flushed warmly across his brain. He let his uncertain legs go, and sat down. 'I – I'm going to bits!' gasped Mr Pope, a pained questioning in the misty blue eyes.

Back in the seclusion of his little room, Tompsett's inevitable 'I told you so!' laughed at him from Tompsett's very mouth. 'I told you so, Pope!' He saw the face, the brutally friendly omniscience in every line. 'I warned you!'

And, for the moment, he gave in. The fight was too much for him. He could not look at supper. He went to bed.

But Tompsett's omniscience followed him there and guessed at his most secret thoughts and half-thoughts. Terrible intrusion this, torturing. Left just this to be said – he had had nowhere else to go. A bachelor clerk of sixty cannot have much in the way of a home or relations to welcome him – and he must go somewhere.

But the country? There was the rub! Had he thought, down in the romantic depths, which never get quite filled up with debris, that he might find a haven of paradisaical rest there? Had he been lured vaguely, without knowing quite what to expect, but hoping – hoping for something he had missed since childhood?

As he tossed about, the bedsheet crawled up to his neck, got into his mouth. He pushed it back violently, as though it were choking him. 'You ought to have had a hobby!' said Tompsett.

Next day and for many days these words of Tompsett's haunted him. He began to hate Tompsett. He watched him pull out ledgers, heard the efficient thud of them on his desk, saw the pages flutter over, felt their texture, studied the names, the columns of figures, greedily. Tompsett had a way of going up a column with deliberate and even strides of his pen. He watched him at it for long spells, fascinated.

Ledgers, the shining desks, the clear briskness of the morning, the lunch hour that came so quickly, the final desk-clearing, the evening paper. A day that went like clockwork, the occasional gossip, the clerical mistakes, the mild scandals – all departmental, intimate. A smoothly running clock, ticking things off to the perfect second. To Mr Pope it suddenly seemed that all that wasn't work, it was – 'a hobby'!

Four mornings thereafter he said to Mrs Gill:

'I'm taking a turn into the city today. Be back last train.'

'That's right, Mr Pope! See you enjoy yourself!'

He flushed as he read the reticence in her eyes which signified he had been moping and should enjoy himself. And the flush held as he went down the little garden, down the road to the city. His legs felt lively, his body lighter, his eyes shone clear of their mistiness. He spoke to no one. He asked for his ticket quietly. He had the fear that someone might guess his insane intention, and the earth would not then conveniently open and swallow him up.

He avoided the haunts of Tompsett and the others, though a sudden access of swagger had tempted him at the lunch hour to revisit the old café. But his caution or fear had prevailed, and at eight o'clock that night he staggered up the garden path, heavy pack on his aching shoulders, not caring whether he had had food that day or not, utterly played out, but excited – with a secret, half-shamed streak of happiness winding in and out the excitement.

Mrs Gill greeted him presently, nodding with a smile at his twinkling eyes; nodding again later when she observed how supper had been dealt with.

'I was just saying to myself as I was sure you would be the better of it,' she said.

'Yes,' said Mr Pope. 'Yes. And, by the way, Mrs Gill, I – I should like breakfast at eight. Knock at twenty to – if – if that would suit you? I've always been used –'

She nodded amply.

'Surely, Mr Pope. It would suit me even better. And habits are habits, as my old mother used to say.'

That evening, until midnight, in the secrecy of his sitting-room, Mr Pope was busy as a criminal, both with the contents of his pack and with his dreams; finally busy with the bottom half of a bookcase which had a lock and key. From midnight he slept like a log, yet at the first knock on his door he was awake. Two minutes he lay, then, throwing back the bed-clothes, he pivoted.

Shaved, dressed, breakfasted, and at 8.15 was toddling down the garden path. At two minutes to nine was toddling up the garden path. At nine prompt he was alone in his sitting-room, breakfast things cleared.

He did not hesitate. Humming a snatch of melody, he went across to the bookcase, and, stooping, pulled out a new, large leather-bound volume. With a gentle thud he deposited it on the writing table before the window. Picking up the black wooden penholder from the somewhat ornamental inkstand, he deftly snicked out the old nib, replacing it with a shining and familiar new one, which he wetted skilfully. Then he set himself before his ledger.

## III

Tompsett, had he seen, would surely have guffawed at length and called upon his gods to strike him pink before the high drama now enacting itself by the little window which looked out upon a garden with two trees and a singing bird.

But whereas Tompsett, by exercise of horse sense, could evade reality in an admirably practical manner, Mr Pope was not so fortunate in his make-up. In these last four days he had *seen* himself as one of the unimaginable army of finally discharged clerks, 'pen-pushers', whom the vast silence and aimlessness of retirement appal at first, then settle down upon as a deadly blight, slowly to stifle, to kill.

Clearly something had to be done about it, and as a realist who possesses, not a hobby but the awful gift of vision, Mr Pope had decided to tackle it in his own way. So perfectly did he know, however, what his old friend Tompsett would think of him, that he had endured short spasms of excruciating agony at his own folly. With the bag of books on his back he had felt like a criminal with his loot. But he had stuck to the loot, and here he was.

For ever since he had consciously listened to the singing birds, his project had been vaguely forming in his mind, and it was to be no mere duplicating of what he had done for over forty years. The set of books was complete, and in the space for the firm's title he had inscribed in beautiful penmanship the name 'Philip Pope.' He had hesitated over clothing the bareness, the naked inadequacy of the name, with an '& Co.' or 'Ltd.', or both. But a conservative sense of the fitness of things had prevailed.

And now, looking up, he heard once more the notes of the bird. Wonderful notes, that sang to the strange thing that was now singing within himself. An extravagant expenditure of notes.... Notes, eh? Golden notes!...

His clients would be, not the meaningless, lifeless names of nearly half a century, but – birds!

He had to get up abruptly from his desk. Oh, monstrous and egregious folly! Oh, madness! He walked about his sitting-room. Myriads of birds, each one of them with his varied and wonderful notes, his inexhaustible stores! What accountancy, what variation, what intricacy of detail, to unravel, to set down, walk by walk, day by day! Madness – sheer! And at last he collapsed from exhaustion – of the body, not of the mind. For the mind went on, working by single and double fantasy, feverishly, wildly.

Presently there was a knock at the door and he jumped guiltily, slamming the ledger shut, and turning in such a way as to hide it. It was Mrs Gill. It was – lunch!

Life had begun again.

That afternoon, the following day, many following days passed as in the vivid tension of a dream. Sun and weather and a cleaner blood brought tan and a faint glow to the parchment cheeks. Until an afternoon came when he went down the road to the little town, and, pulling himself together, entered the library.

She was a young woman, the lady behind the counter, with dark hair over a pale forehead, dark attractive eyes, an expressive oval face. She smiled at Mr Pope, a slow quiet smile. He felt unaccountably drawn, and cleared his throat.

'I want a book,' he managed.

She waited.

'About birds,' he amplified. For he had come to realise the pressing necessity for inquiry into the credentials of his clients.

'This is the catalogue, but – your ticket?'

Mr Pope hadn't a ticket. Well, he couldn't get a book without a ticket. Did he live?...

'Yes, I stay with Mrs Gill up the road.'

Then it would be quite simple. He would fill up this form, get Mrs Gill and another householder to sign it, and bring it back. Then a ticket would be issued.

'Thank you very much,' said Mr Pope. He hesitated uncertainly, as though the kindness in the dark eyes were as mesmeric as helpful.

'If you are anxious to get a book now – well, I could give you one, if you'd be sure to come back with the form at once. Bird books are not often asked for.'

'Thank you very much, but – not at all. I – I'll get the form. Shouldn't like –'

'That's all right.' She handed him the catalogue.

He began to fumble through it. She saw his uncertainty and, quietly leaving the desk, returned with four volumes.

'Perhaps one of these – '

His gratitude made him momentarily inarticulate. One volume, with rather beautiful coloured plates, completed his silence. He caught at it.

'Your number,' she said, turning from a ledger, 'will be 2701. I'll note that now, if you give me your full name.'

He left the library with a supreme sense of the beneficence of life; and returned within the hour, form duly completed.

'I am very grateful to you,' he said, and their eyes met and smiled.

Every day saw his gratitude grow deeper. Spring was in full spate. Bird singing had become individual competitions in ecstasy. Mr Pope was surely the busiest man within a vast radius. For his clients were busy, extraordinarily busy, and miraculously elusive. Moreover, the coloured plates, gorgeous as they were, were often baffling. The different finches, for example; the tits. He mopped, he followed, he crawled. He listened, he watched, he studied. And out of chaos came, little by little, order. Seeing nothing, and from the evidence of his ears only, 'Ah, a robin!' he would pronounce, with nodding pride, '*not* a wren.'

The difference between blackbird music and thrush music baffled him for a time. He was frequently making mistakes. Until at last – he noted down, after a sweating struggle for adequate words, certain characteristics. And that was the beginning of a thrilling new interest.

Slowly the ledger grew to exhibit the most curious patch-work of figures and haphazard paragraphs.

'The starling,' wrote Mr Pope, 'is not to be trusted. He

draws on various accounts not his own. He is a forger and a mocker. Today I thought my new friend, the stone-breaker, had shifted his stance. But I was wrong. A glossy, speckled starling was guilty of impersonating. I must see if Miss Storey has any book on the starling in her library. I hope she does not consider my frequent visits a trouble. I thought last time I called upon her that she looked weary. I hope nothing is worrying. For the world is beautiful in a way that I was quite unaware of hitherto. How extremely withdrawn is Tompsett!'

And when he had written the paragraph, each sentence having first been carefully 'tried out', he read it over and over, and glowed with the absorbing reality of it – yet finding space in his secretive pleasure to hope the best for Miss Storey and to twist a flick of pity at Tompsett.

Wonderful life, wonderful account keeping. His leg muscles were positively developing; his health, his sense of well-being as he had never known it.

And life was not only wonderful: it was cram-full of adventures, even adventures of the most physical. For in the case of the bird there are three distinguishing features: song, plumage, and egg. And in such new exercises as tree-climbing, Mr Pope found difficulty. Behold him, for example, waiting on the dusk, skulking home by field and hedgerow, and being – for luck is not always kind – encountered by Mrs Gill in the garden. The sidling, the retreating backwards, the fatal tripping over the doorstep, so that the guardian hand is dislodged from a position astern where a deadly rent ran the full curvature....

The wonder is he did not some time expire from over-hasty acceleration of his untried heart. Life was a debauch.

And the spring went on. And the birds had even less conscience than Mr Pope. From the silvery pinnacle of the dawn to the hushed hollows of evening they pursued their aerial arabesques, their flashing riotous loves, their nest-building and singing, their spring madness.

Enter the cuckoo. And Mr Pope 'skipped' lunch.

At the library, which he reached ten minutes before closing time, Miss Storey assured his slightly dishevelled *empressement* that there was quite a literature on the cuckoo.

Mr Pope licked his lips. It was as he thought; he could rely on her.

Ah, more than rely on her, for here he touched a simplicity, a vision, to which he was at home. Perhaps a too fatal understanding in her eyes, her dark, soft eyes. Something a little too soft about her, something, also as he had previously noted, increasingly 'worrying,' troubled, as though the darkness of the eye had got ringed by an outer faint-blue darkness.

But he missed the uneasy note altogether as he almost staggered from the library. For his mind was aflame. His shrunken body soared above its staggerings; while his lips muttered, over and over, what her lips had spoken, as, with a smile, she had laid a volume or two before him – 'The cuckoo told his name to all the hills.' She had introduced him to the poets!

It was too much. Too much at one fell swoop. 'The cuckoo told his name to all the hills'!... 'Oh, my God!' said Mr Pope in the throes of a divine agony. And he abandoned himself to a green mound on the uplands beyond Mrs Gill's. There, hugging his knees like the very shrunken ghost of a long-dead Viking, he gazed stonily down upon the winding river-belt, where all day long he had hunted –

> 'No bird, but an invisible thing,
> A voice, a mystery....'

And suddenly there came floating up to him in soft mellow mockery, 'Cuck-oo! cuck-oo!'

But fortunately for Mr Pope it was the sort of debauchery that Nature permits, and she saw to it that his slumbers were profound.

## IV

Meantime the affairs of the firm were getting into a somewhat muddled state. Time that the managing owner held some sort of solid stock-taking to see more or less where he stood. Some weeks passed in this onerous occupation. Knowledge had to be detailed and precise. A rather formidable Latin nomen-

clature presented a difficulty, but his mind had had always
that love of orderliness and precision which is of the essence of
true scholarship. Figures and paragraphs gave way for some
pages to trees that were charts of orders, families, sub-
families, genera. Beyond doubt an indigestible business, dry –
but curiously prideful. 'Ah, the robin,' Mr Pope would nod,
'*Erithacus rubecula*.' Whereupon a small lump would roll up
from his heart to his throat.

Such pride might be held by many to be the beginning of the
end – if not of all things, at least of the poets, of the magic.

But within a week he was back at the paragraph again, at
this paragraph:

'A kingfisher and a grey wagtail – in one day! The firm
totters on the brink of insolvency. I have found the ravishment
of this day the severest yet. The grey wagtail *hovered*. I can say
no more. It was a space between trees by the edge of the
stream, a space of sunlight between green. And he hovered
with the sun on him. When he went, I crawled to the edge of
the stream to rest there. And as I rested, lo! there came upon
me, darting up-stream, a living blue-green jewel. A kingfisher
– no other! And was gone. It was too much in such a short
space of time, and it was accordingly late before I reached the
library, where I hadn't been for some time. Consider my
surprise to find another in Miss Storey's place. I am afraid I
must have shown even stupefaction. I know it took my slow
mind some time to understand that she was gone for good. It
meant that she would never come back. Moreover, there was
a look on the face of the thin, elderly woman in her place, a
shrewish look, so that I am left with the feeling that I crept
from her presence – certainly without asking for a book. A
kingfisher, a grey wagtail – and Miss Storey gone. I do not
know what to think. I cannot plan.'

Mr Pope's mind became a jumble. From his pleasure in the
use of the word 'ravishment' (a recent acquisition) to the
disturbing knowledge of Miss Storey's departure, his mind
jumped about aimlessly. He became restless. It took him very
much longer than usual to fall asleep. Moreover, he dreamed.
And in his dreams Miss Storey's face got mixed up with the

face of a little boy who had climbed a tree for him some days before. In his dreams they were nesting together, he and the little boy who was also Miss Storey. The partnership was perfect; for the little fellow had keen eyes and climbed like a sailor; while Mr Pope imparted his knowledge with a wonderful and thrilling skill, consciously (if pridefully) suppressing the Latin, but most aptly laying a casual finger on the poets.

His eloquence awoke him before his time; and in his disillusionment he tossed about. But in due course he pulled himself together, and got up purposefully. He was in the act of drawing on his trousers when he heard voices by the garden gate.

'The wanton!' came cutting feminine tones. 'She with her college training and all her orders! Corrupting ...' But Mr Pope, who had been balancing precariously on one leg, overbalanced, and by the time he had got his legs disentangled Mrs Gill was sighing:

'Ah, well, the poor thing – '

'Poor thing, indeed!'

'I mean,' began Mrs Gill hurriedly, 'I mean – '

But her visitor had apparently no great interest in Mrs Gill's meanings.

'It's just what I warned them. And that's for the vicar! And she won't open her mouth, the hussy! And even before she came here she must ...' The high-pitched voice choked. 'I don't know how she could have had the face!'

'The vicar's in for a rough time,' thought Mr Pope to himself with a whiff of the old departmental humour, as Miss Grainger minced off down the road, her thin nostrils no doubt scenting battles from afar. She was an elderly maiden lady, an active worker for the Church Militant.

But this intrusion of worldly bitterness did not help Mr Pope's restlessness. Indeed, it increased it. 'Interests,' human or Tompsettian, had never been his strong point. And now that Miss Storey should have failed him, leaving a grey wagtail and a kingfisher on his hands ... it was – it was 'wanton.' The unexpected word banished utterly any wry flicker of humour, hung itself up in his mind, stared upon him. Of course, it was

Miss Grainger's word! His mind had merely reproduced it, as his mind was getting into the habit of doing with words that struck him as new and arresting.

But the word stuck all through breakfast. It was not merely arresting: it was sly and sinister. It mocked him. It could tell him a thing or two – if he would give it the chance! It leered at him round odd corners of his mind. It dared him. But he was loyal to Miss Storey. The association was colossally preposterous. 'And yet ... ' leered Miss Grainger's word; leered Miss Grainger herself.

Even the bacon lost its savour, and Mr Pope set forth under half ballast, so that his journeyings became fitful and purposeless. There were no entries made in the ledger. No new observations.

At supper-time his voice suddenly took command of him and said to Mrs Gill, who was 'clearing':

'I see Miss Storey has left the library.'

Mrs Gill looked at him in a certain way.

'Yes,' she said. 'Yes.'

But now he could say no more.

'I suppose you heard?' said Mrs Gill, lingering.

'No.'

'It's all the talk. Miss Grainger's hot on it.' She paused. 'There wasn't an inkling beforehand.'

'What – what was it, Mrs Gill?'

'She's had a baby,' said Mrs Gill.

Mr Pope's jaw dropped.

'No one noticed anything,' said Mrs Gill.

In a wild search for something to say, Mr Pope heard words forming conversationally in his brain to the effect that he had not noticed anything himself. But they remained unspoken.

Mrs Gill lingered.

And he knew that she lingered with expectations of discussing the matter, simply and to the point, as folk of their age should. A sensation of lockjaw held his mouth.

'She hasn't been here that long; just nigh on eight months,' said Mrs Gill.

He got his head to nod with what seemed a ponderous stroke.

'And she won't tell nothing,' concluded Mrs Gill.

Then after lingering a little longer with no noticeable encouragement, she went.

His body allowed its freedom, his mind a full rein, he gave
himself up to a monstrous wonder. Between the chairs, round
the table, up and down he went, breath held, breath hissing in
prolonged escapements through his teeth, astounded, incredu-
lous, yet conscious of a sensation that linked him somehow
with the incredible happening itself. Twice he barked his
shins. But if thought could follow no rational paths, vision
became ever clearer, particularly a near vision of Miss Storey's
face. It fascinated him. It drew him.

Until he realised his own helplessness, his futile age. A
withered little marionette figure, performing his daily tricks
on the parchment surfaces of life. How unreal before that
maelstrom of the dark currents of the blood!

But far at the back of his mind a new cunning had been born
of the birds. He was not giving in. Not even for Miss Storey.
Call me an idiot, call me a sentimental old fool, but I'm not
giving in, said Mr Pope in bitter wrath to the self inside him.

## V

Some weeks later, Mr Pope, instead of stretching carpet
slippers to the evening fire, changed them, as he had done the
two previous nights, for boots. He had the aspect of a man
preparing for a very special board-room conference.

Carefully he studied the waning light from the window and
plainly adjudged the darkness not yet near enough for his
departure. Drawing forth a ledger, he read over what had been
last posted therein. He read it again, lingering here and there,
lingering particularly over the concluding sentences, '... so
that the darkness has its greatness equally with the light; and
in many ways surpasses it, for there is a mystery and gathering
together of thought in which the body sits as still as a deep
pool...'

Presently he set forth, heart throbbing a little, body keyed
up, and in due course found himself by the belt of trees that

wound with the river. For some ten minutes he held steadily on an upward course until, coming by a certain pathway as landmark, he struck into the enveloping darkness of the tree-belt. Hands outstretched, he groped onwards, slowly, care-fully, until the grey-glooming stillness of a silent river pool drew him up. He recognised a special tree-trunk, and, feeling for a small heap of dried bracken at its foot, he sat upon it and waited.

And it came in the end – the song of the nightingale!

Crouched over his knees, eyes on the profundities of the pool, he delivered himself to that song. And, as though con-scious of the inarticulate soul of the listener, the singer gave of his magical best.

Gave too much for the frail human vessel at the tree-foot to hold, so that a drowsy numbness caught at Mr Pope's spirit and sank it Lethe-wards as though of hemlock he had drunk....

Until the moon, newly risen, caught the darkness and the spirit in a glimmering net, and drew the freight, meshed in white witchery, to shores in faëry lands forlorn.....

Echoes of poetry and lovely meaninglessness, travailed groping....

Abruptly the song ceased. There were scattering of branches on the outer edge of the tree-belt, a body brushing its way through, a whimpering suddenly stilled.

Mr Pope came back to the river bank and the grey-glooming pool, startled ears straining to altogether earthly sounds. Nearer, nearer, coming straight for him, till at last there glided in upon him the hooded form of a woman carrying something at her breast, till the moonlight caught at the pallor under the hood and revealed to the eyes of Mr Pope the undoubted features of Miss Storey.

Twisted up and stiffened, not unlike a malformed tree-stump himself, he crouched there, all volition gone, gaping, grotesque.

Her hood slipped from her hair. No sound came from her, and like some fateful figure in a preordained tragedy, in whom emotion and life had played out their parts, she turned to the grey-glooming pool.

One step she took – two – and Mr Pope had her by the shoulder.

He was gasping now, but the face that looked at him hardly showed any emotion. Slowly from his grip the figure sank down.

'Miss Storey!' said Mr Pope, slipping down beside her. 'Miss Storey!' he cried, putting an arm around her and drawing her up against his heart. 'Miss Storey – my God!' gulped Mr Pope.

'Ah, why?' she muttered.

Why, indeed! By God, just in the nick of time! His heart began to whir with a wild, mad exultation. Why, indeed, eh? In the very nick! The child began to cry.

Victory did not come at once, but when at last he had made it plain that he would not leave go of her now for all the entreaties on earth, nor yet though the heavens came down in very small bits, she suddenly crumpled in his hands, her body shaken in a convulsion of frightful coughing.

He got her to her feet ultimately, made her grip at an arm of his, while head down he burrowed forward into the branch entanglements, holding the child with both hands against his chest; a masterful progress, wherein he felt himself not only commanding life but ordering destiny.

But that night destiny, in the person of the doctor, entered his little sitting-room and said quietly:

'She won't last very long.'

There was a silence in which Mr Pope's mind groped blindly. Then –

'Won't – last – very long,' he repeated.

The doctor eyed him, and his expression softened. He shook his head. Did not know what she had been doing. Delirious. Temperature 105, no reserve – impossible – utterly.

And Mr Pope made a supreme effort at self-command.

'And the child?' he asked.

'All right,' said the doctor. Then after a little – 'I'll get some things – be back in a few minutes – but – ' He shrugged.

Mr Pope accompanied him down the little garden to the gate.

'You – you'll spare no expense, doctor? I – I'll – ' His voice broke.

## VI

Mr Pope sat at his desk in the little sitting-room gazing down the garden where spring had blown into summer. Events had justified the doctor, and Mr Pope in a brief space had played many parts. Summer was also blowing its flowers where tragedy lay asleep with its own secrets for evermore.

But what at that moment was most definitely impinging upon Mr Pope's consciousness was no more than a phrase in a dead tongue. Though for that matter the phrase pulsed with more life than any phrase of the only living tongue which Mr Pope knew. And it spelt – *In loco parentis.*

With it he had satisfied (very easily, it is true) some one or two relatives of Miss Storey, with whom he had come perforce in contact, there being neither father nor mother.

*In loco parentis.* What a starting-place for vision! The Psalmist certainly owed him ten more years. But, with care, why not twenty? Why not more? Thraldom of birds and woods and the ancient earth, of dark and mysterious blood currents, of wonder, of gratitude, of sorrow, of joy, of love.

Let Tompsett make an accountancy of life in beer and bowls and be happy. Mr Pope had to think of his own future, had to train pliant limbs to shin up trees for him. What a naturalist he would make of him! And the expeditions to-gether! Down the bright avenues of spring days, in the hushed summer woods, in the mellow autumn, to the long winter evenings for reading and preparation!

His finger-tips clutched spasmodically at the ledger which for so many weeks had lain unopened; presently caught a cover and turned it over, revealing a front page on which had been inscribed the firm's name of Philip Pope. His eyes, with the haze of vision on them, came from the garden to the open page, regarded the name, the ever-bare, inadequate name. A moment, and the eyes were brimming once more with the light of adventure, and in the heart of it glowed a wise pagan humour, a final self-mocking altogether delicious, while the hand, dipping pen-point in inkpot, proceeded with practised care to extend the name to: Philip Pope & Son.

# Strath Ruins

*Chambers's Journal, 1927*

He sat so still that a dipper landed on a flat stone in the stream three yards from his boots and bobbed a white waistcoat as in merry greeting. On the opposite bank rabbits went leisurely about their business of clipping the grass to a carpet of matchless texture. Above the outcrop of rock against which he leaned stood a clump of hazel, and now suddenly from a swinging wand dropped upon his ears the plaintive, liquid notes of a robin's song.

Something of exquisite reverie in the robin's meditation gave the September afternoon, the hazel-trees, the lichened croft-ruin on the flat opposite, the drowse of the burn, the whole strath, an air of olden dreaming, of remoteness in time and space, to which his spirit responded. While the dipper ploughed the shallows that got lost in the pool round the corner, he stared with filming eyes, so that the stones in the river, the narrow flat beyond, the hillside of trees beyond that, sank back into an infinite perspective of the great silent places of the world, where he had adventured and risked and had had his being these last thirty years. Nights under the moon in the Australian hinterland; mesmeric flashing of wastes of amethyst; finds of gold and silver and precious stones marked on maps that for one reason or another were never used; Alaska; the Rockies, with that staggering all-in picture of himself.

A little place, this strath, with the air about it of a tale that is told, its wild adventuring done, haunted now by night echoes of curlews like the crying of lost souls on the wind; hedged about, too, like a veritable cemetery under the jealous

care of gamekeepers and gamelaws. Not a royal ending to a
story of old Gaelic blood that was as royal and brave and fine
as any in the history of our little spinning globe. The passing of
that spirit could be felt by one sitting thus calmly; was felt
surely, too, by the very stones in the burn, so dreamily
hypnotic the monotone they drew from the soft peat water;
and by the trees, so still they were; by the sunlight, so flaked
and yellow; by the old lichened stones of the ruin become at
last a cairn. The hearthstone of the Gael! ... and great ones
who made money (which is power) out of patent medicines
and sauces and boots came and lorded it ...

His woodsman's attention was instantly focused by a sudden change in the attitude of the rabbits. They had all ceased
eating. Presently one loped quietly away towards the warren
at the hill-foot, then another, until the flat was alive with
them. At their front doors they paused, sitting up on hind-legs
as if expressing a word or two of mild disapproval, before
condescending finally to disappear. There came the soft thudding of human footsteps descending the braeside of trees
which sloped steeply above the listener by the rock.

The tanned face of the listener did not move, though a
quickening came to the eyes, a keenness to the expression. Did
not much matter to him who it might be, only he did not want
it to be the keepers. For the rest, long experience had taught
him the wonderful invisibility of immobility, and his rock-
grey suit and greying hair were good enough protective colouring.

By leaning forward he could glimpse through a root-outcrop
of hazel twigs, overhanging the three feet of rock he sat
against, a fair slice of a fair-sized pool. The water in the pool
was black, because it came from the far peat-moss, and
because the pool was deep. All sound of footsteps had ceased,
but the listener had the sensation of eyes scanning the pool
from the near side, which he himself could not command. It
must be one of the keepers.

It wasn't one of the keepers, however, for presently footsteps sounded on the rocky ledge above, coming down to a

final ledge, which jutted out into the pool, giving its neck a snake-twist. This ledge was under direct observation, and the young fellow who proceeded to flatten himself upon it was plainly no keeper or gillie.

The deliberate, wary carefulness of his actions was something to behold; the poise, the tense expectancy. The stranger by the rock-face watched with fascination. Anchored precariously to the narrow shelf, at last the young man got head and shoulders balancing out over the water; down towards the water. For long seconds he remained as though petrified, the water touching the forehead, the eyes plainly trying to fathom the dark deeps.

The face drew back, uplifted, flushed with blood, water trickling unheeded from black hair on the temples. But the eyes were alert, the lips tight. He remained for a second on all fours on the ledge, peering at a thought in his mind; nodded; noiselessly withdrew.

It might easily have been a scene in the wilds, and the stranger waited with a flickering smile of content about his alert features, a warmth about his heart. For, though the ways of birds and reptiles and animals, of all wild things, held a deep appeal, the ways of man in the wild were irresistible.

His ears were presently rewarded by the faint click of a snapping branch. The smile deepened, knowingly; and it was with the utmost precaution he made sure of the slit in the root-growth as an invisible loophole.

The slim hazel branch which the young fellow brought with him was fully eight feet long, and on the point of it was a thin barbed hook somewhat less in size than a crooked forefinger. Plainly the operation was to be of the most delicate. The face under the lash of dark hair was now pale, drawn somewhat with excitement. Each movement held a reserve of strength, and the balancing and anchoring again of the body was an exercise in nice adjustments which the stranger expertly appreciated.

The rod began to go down, steadily down, the forehead lapping the water as before, the eyes peering, slowly down, down. A pause – lengthening itself out; infinitely delicate movements of the hand that held the rod, as though it were groping fearfully; a sudden utter immobility; a swift fierce strike upwards; the body springing on to all fours; a swirling and smashing of a great silvery fish; the just perceptible break in the rhythmic upheave as the young man got to his feet – and the fish was gone.

The stranger's face, narrowing, reflected the expression of intense disappointment which now held the young man, unmoving, to the rocky ledge. Slow, automatic, was the examination of the hook, the look around the pool with its invisible bottom. No move, no surface swirl. Suddenly he leapt from the ledge and was gone.

The stranger waited, uncertain. But he had not to wait long. The faint splash of a body taking the water, and swimming into view came the dark head, a stick, half the length of the first, carried crosswise between the teeth.

A determined young riever! And in a moment the riever had plainly got bottom beyond the rocky ledge and not far from the farther side. Manifestly not a smooth bottom, however, for the gleaming shoulders bobbed uncertainly, once, indeed, the head going out of sight altogether. A boulder it must be, and obviously the toes were feeling for a soft yielding side under the boulder.

The instant contact was made the stranger knew, reading the expression of the face in the water with more than certainty. And for quite a time the dark head made no definite resolution, plainly having delivered itself up to sensations elusively but exquisitely pleasurable.

Bobbing there like a cork, the toes touching and smoothing and caressing the yielding, invisible satin-silver of the king of fish … a delicate flirtation, thought the stranger, but wondering vaguely how it could be more.

He found out quickly enough. The gaff began to travel down the naked body, until the arm was fully extended. The head lay back; there was a slight hissing expulsion of breath, and the head disappeared.

A moment, and the surface was a lashing froth. Clearly the young riever knew every invisible foothold of his ground. Man and fish reached the water's edge; a swirl, a clean heave, and the fish was high and dry, smashing and walloping the stones in frenzied efforts to reach its native element again, while its would-be captor, thrown wildly of his balance by the heave, had been launched backwards into the pool.

All too clearly the fish would have won, had not the stranger, with remarkable agility, leapt across the shallows, nailed the slithering body with a boot on the water's edge, and fallen upon it. Fingers found the gills, and a smart rap on the back of the head with the edge of a flat stone finished matters. 'A near thing!' he said, and turned.

The head in the water was the head of a river god caught in un-translatable surprise, with no room even for dismay. But surprise quickly faded into harsh, silent suspicion, brows gathering.

The stranger's smile, however, did not fade, and the blue eyes which regarded the gathering hostility were unfaltering in their clear steadiness, a compelling clarity of blue. Indeed, there was something in that straight look which delicately but unswervingly demanded acknowledgment. The figure in the water stirred. 'Thanks,' he mumbled.

The stranger's smile deepened to friendliness, to a friendly keenness. 'This isn't the first chap you struck – there, by the ledge. No scar. He must still be at large.'

'He is.'

'Where, do you think?'

'He'll settle again by the ledge.'

'No?'

'Yes.'

'Very well. If you slip across, I'll take this chap over.' And picking the fish up, the stranger started across.

But the naked figure came ashore, and was quickly survey-ing the salmon's very successful efforts in scattering innumer-able glistening scales about the stones. After a rapid, keen-eyed survey of the surrounding strath, he stooped to the stones and performed certain obliterating rites with gravel and sand; then, taking to the water again, was in a second or two beside his clothes.

The stranger had studied these actions with appraising eye, and now as the young man appeared beside him at the pool's neck, remarked, 'He's a beauty!'

The young riever studied the fish, nodded. 'Ay, fourteen pounds.' And immediately lifting the glistening body, swung it up into a narrow rock crevice behind. Whereupon, with exhaustive care, he proceeded to cover it up, until no single scale remained anywhere visible.

'Would take a lot of finding now,' reckoned the stranger.

'Keeps the bluebottles from getting at him as well.'

The young man went and washed his hands in the stream, came back. 'Well, that's that!'

'You 'll leave him there until –?'

'The road's clear.'

'I see.'

There was a pause. Then the riever threw the stranger a look. 'Unless you would like your share now?'

The stranger saw the friendliness struggling with a questioning awkwardness. 'What about having a shot at the first chap again – with another, we could have one each?'

Still the riever hesitated.

'I'm a visitor to these parts,' continued the stranger. 'But – I know the penalties. And – you can rely on me.'

They faced each other a silent moment; then the dark mistrustful face broke into a swift, merry friendliness. 'Right! They're after me, you know. Always after me. If I'm copped – there will be no mercy at all.' He paused, and regarded the stranger with a sudden, searching keenness. 'Tell me – how did you come on me like yon, so – so –?'

'Unexpectedly? I've been sitting by the rock here for some hours back, studying the wild life of the place. It's a hobby of mine!'

'I see.' Then, 'I could have bet anything in the world that no living human being was within half-a-mile of me. Of course, I knew none of the keepers was here.'

'Quite!' nodded the stranger.

And suddenly a mysterious friendliness was swirling about them, inducing an awkwardness which the older man broke with a quite eager, 'Well, what about the other chap?'

'If you think you'll risk it. After all, a glass may be on us from any one of those hill-edges. There is no such a thing as absolute certainty.'

'There never is in life,' considered the stranger; 'at least, not in the interesting, fine things.'

'Come on, then! But first I'll take a run up to the top to see if I can see anything. I should have been up before this, because there's a fold in the strath between the top and the far-down flats. Wait a minute!'

While this scouting operation was under way the stranger approached the ledge on his own account, and, after much wriggling and precarious balancing, got anchored; but when at last he got his forehead to the water, his eyes encountered nothing but impenetrable gloom.

He hung on fixedly, and gradually the water gathered a sunny, mote-spangled, brown-gold luminosity, that was penetrable, however, only for a short distance. Of a river-bottom he could see no slightest trace. He lifted his head to ease his breathing.

'Is he there?' came from above.

The stranger half-twisted round. 'Blest if I can see anything at all!'

'I know. But look steadily for the bottom close by the rock, and you'll see a thing like a dark shadow away down.'

The stranger got into position again, and for a long time was utterly motionless. Then he twisted round, getting up on hands and knees. 'I see a dark waving shadow about the length of a sea-trout – sometimes.'

'That's him! Fifteen pounds, if he's an ounce!'

'No?'

'Yes.'

'By gosh! I've done a bit hunting in my time out abroad, but rarely such delicate game as this!'

The young man laughed. 'Good enough sport.'

'It is.' Then reflectively, 'I say, don't they fish for 'em?'

'No! No use! Wouldn't look at anything, though you tried till you were black in the face. The first drop of spate and they're off. They're waiting for it.'

'I see. And do you never try anything besides that small hook?'

'No.'

'So if they didn't lie at the ledge here, or out at that stone, you wouldn't manage?'

'Oh, yes!'

'How?'

'I'd make them lie.'

A pause while the older man studied an enigmatic smile; then he shrugged. 'I give it up. You've got your stick ready? Good; come along, then!'

'Would you like a shot?'

'What?'

'You have a shot at him if you like. If you could manage to hook him, I'd sling him clear on the upheave without stopping. It's when you give him time to get a grip of the water while you're getting to your own feet that's the fatal time.'

'I'll never manage!'

'Have a shot.'

'Eh? Really?' A faint excitement was evident.

'Yes, go on! Turn the hook towards the rock before you put it down, because, of course, you soon lose sight of it. Touch bottom out beyond him a little; then gradually work the stick in along the bottom – until you feel him. Do it very gently, and he won't mind you touching him at all. You'll feel him sort of moving with the water and touching the stick. When you're sure in this way that you're right under him, strike straight up. Keep your eye on the shadow.'

And the stranger allowed himself to be persuaded. 'Righto! But you'll forgive me if I mess it!'

He followed instructions as well as he could, his heart misgiving him every foot he went deeper. At long last the stick grounded with a jar. He lost sight of the shadow altogether. What an impossible hope! Was that it there again – the wavering, dim shadow? Oh, most futile, wild business! ... Inch by blind inch... and then suddenly something touched his stick. Every muscle stiffened. It touched his stick again.

'If he's touching you, time your strike to a touch.'

Clear – touch; clear – touch; clear – strike!

Curse, he had missed! but before the exclamation had right formed in his mind the stick was snatched from his hand, there was a swirling surface smashing, and a silver body hurtling over his head. He scrambled from the ledge. The young man had the quarry between his knees, and was saying, 'Don't know how you did it; it's almost through his tail!'

'By gosh! I thought I had missed him!'

'I know. You feel no weight to begin with. A bonny fish.'

'A beauty!'

'We'll put him beside the other –'

The cracking of a twig, and the young man's face underwent an appalling change. 'My God!' and he had the stranger by the arm, dragging him fiercely. 'This way!'

'Hi! Hi! You there!' sang out the voice of an invisible body bearing down heavily.

'For your life, come on! Rory – the head-keeper. Hell! This way!'

The stranger, for all his greying hair, had a remarkably nimble pair of feet. 'You go on!' he hissed to the young man. 'Save yourself!'

'No d— fear! This way!' And then after a further hundred yards, 'Now – down there with you – and lie flat! He'll follow me. I'll shake him off.' And the stranger got a push which very effectively sent him 'down there' to cover behind a tangled, bush-matted outcrop of rock. The bellowing mass of the head-keeper went crashing past, shouting at the fugitive in front and cursing the sleek, correctly trained spaniel at his heels, that plainly was at a complete loss to know what was required of him.

The stranger crept back towards the pool, found the salmon, very carefully hid it in the crevice by the other fish, got into the hillside of trees, and continued his way silently downward, a small smile flickering about his quickened breathing. A splendid little adventure. The old free spirit might be twisted into poaching ways, but it breathed, thank God! He would get into touch with the young riever again, who could risk a generous gesture even in the hour of danger.

His eyes lit up; the smile deepened enigmatically. A real poaching raid can have its thrills.

The face of Rory Mackenzie, the head-keeper, iron autocrat of glens and moor, was dark with the repressed vastness of his wrath, when late that same evening he stamped in upon two figures by the corner of the dog-kennels below the second keeper's house. The second keeper, Angus Mathieson, heard his coming ere yet he had turned the peat-stack, and had abruptly interrupted the *ceilidh* with his neighbour, Willie, the crofter-gillie.

'Begod, that's Rory! – and something's up!' Both men stiffened in expectancy.

Plainly something was up, but Rory did not come at it immediately.

'It's a fine night,' said Willie cannily.

'It's all that!' agreed Rory in thick mockery. It was his privilege to speak his mind at his pleasure.

Willie, checked, cleared his throat to show he was not checked.

'Ay, it's all that,' pursued Rory; 'but what I'd like to know is what the defil we're all coming to, what the defil we're getting paid our wages for, and what the defil is the use of doing anything at all!'

He spat emphatically upon the earth, paced a yard or two, growled rumblingly, paused starkly to proceed: 'I got him as clean as any man was ever gotten. I had him nailed in the act. I came up on him. I had him under my feet!'

He glared on the under-keeper, who showed proper astonishment, but kept his mouth shut.

'Don Mackay!' exploded Rory.

The name certainly had its effect.

'You're saying that!' whispered Willie.

'Yes, that's what I'm saying. For all the years he's been at it no one of you could lay a hand on him. But I got him! He ran me for nearly a mile, but I got him in the end, sitting, if you please, as calm as a cock sparrow.

'"You've got me, Rory," he says.

'"D— your impudence, I have!" says I.

'"You wouldn't have got me if I hadn't burst my ankle," he says.

'"Oh, indeed!" says I. "I have you now anyway, and you'll d— well pay for that same!"'

Rory took a turn up and down; the excitement of the hunt was coming back on him, when Willie suddenly asked, 'Did he have anything on him?'

Rory looked upon him in heaviest scorn. 'It was likely he would be carrying seven or six salmon, and me chasing him!'

But it was in backing out that Willie seemed to put his foot in it properly. 'No, not likely, when you come to think on't! I mean he would have left them by the pool.'

'He left them where he left them!' exploded Rory with unaccountable wrath. 'If you go to the rock-pool you'll see enough scales to satisfy you, perhaps, if you'll not believe me! Do you understand that I saw the fish thrown and it dancing alive on the rock?'

'I see,' said Willie; but he knew, and the underkeeper knew, that in some mysterious and exasperating way Rory had not found the fish – though he had got everything else, including the elusive Don Mackay. But plainly that was not the main cause of Rory's tortured wrath now. The detection would be sound enough for any court. Trust Rory for that. They discreetly waited Rory's pleasure.

'So I left him with his ankle, and took my way back home by the pool, where – where I completed my evidence. I sent young Alasdair to search by the pool for the salmon that would be hidden besides. He will have them by this time, I make no doubt.'

There was a heavy sarcasm in the last words, implying, enigmatically, that it no longer mattered whether young Alasdair had them or not. And at last the question was born in the minds of his listeners: Had Rory been to the big house, and had the laird not shown his satisfaction deeply enough? Hardly thinkable – but manifestly a conjecture that could explain much.

'So I dressed myself and prepared to set out so that I might

call on the laird himself after he would have had his dinner.
Yes, I thought it over and I said to myself that the importance
of the case was of such a nature that it would have to be visited
with all the full power of the law. He has taken more fish off
the river than everyone in the place and all the gents themselves combined into one. He has that. And you need never tell
me that he stopped at fish!

'So I was shown in. He was nice enough. I'll say that for
him. "Sit down," he says, "and have a cigar." And he pushed
across a box of them to me.

'"What's worrying you now?" he asks.

'And at that I told him the whole thing from the beginning.
I missed nothing. How for years we had been trying to catch
that poacher; what a danger he was to the place; what an
example to the young growing ones, when we had spared no
efforts in doing our duty by way of stamping out, without
quarter, all poaching whatever; how we had laid plans for him
and sat up all night; how he had come to have all the people on
his side, and them covering him up and most like laughing at
us up their sleeves, making out to be always most civil and
polite at the same time. Oh, I went into it – all of it. And then
to-day – how I at last had caught him.

'He took me up at that; most interested, as you would say.
Asked me about my evidence; what I had seen. I admitted that
in a way I had been helped by a chance, but then, in another
way, not by a chance at all, for I had come out to do a quiet
patrol, and from the crest of the ridgie yonder had gotten a
sudden glimpse of his figure on the stone ledges throwing his
fish. I made down through the trees without waiting another
second to look, for he's as slippery as an eel. He bolted, but I
told how I had come up with him in the race, and how he had
admitted he had been caught red-handed.

'At that he passed me the decanter full of whisky. "Fill your
glass," he says. I did so, glad that our work could be so taken
account of.

'And then, "What will we do now?" he asks me. And d—
me if it didn't come at me so suddenly some way as to make me
miss my mouth with the whisky. What would we do now, eh?

What would we do now? I laughed.

'"That's a good joke, if you'll excuse me," I says; "and you'll excuse me spilling the whisky too." The breast of my shirt was wet with it. What would we do now!

'But, begod, the joke was that he meant it! I told him I would write full particulars to Factor Maclean and pay him a visit at such time as would suit him. This was to be the most important prosecution for years, and we would press for the very heaviest penalties. I knew my business, and, this being the very first of its kind in his time, I thought I'd do myself the honour of laying it before him in person.

'He filled up my glass. He was nice enough in a way, as I say. And then he began to ask me about this Don Mackay. Did he sell the fish? No, he didn't sell the fish, I told him, because most likely he couldn't. The place was not that rich that it could be buying salmon! Hardly that! ... What did he do with it then? ... Gave it to any old woman or neighbour for his own reasons – perhaps so that they could laugh up their sleeves; them getting salmon as though they were born to it without paying a halfpenny.

'"They'll pay their rents," he says.

'"You'll know that best yourself," I says. D— me, but I was beginning not to catch his drift at all. And then he says, "So you think we should prosecute?"

'Think! I glared on him. Was it that he was making fun of me?' Rory paused.

Rory paused; eyed the under-keeper, the crofter-gillie. When he proceeded his voice had gathered a desperate calm. 'He said that, taking everything into account, he was not prepared to – to signalise – that was his word – to signalise his entry upon the position of laird by a prosecution!'

The under-keeper shifted his stance; Willie cleared his throat at length.

'It brought a coldness out on me. I looked him in the eye. "Sir," I replied, "it is your right to do what you like with your estate and with us, your servants, and our labours, but what you have just said, if it could be heard by him, your brother –

if I may so mention him – would be enough to make him turn in his grave!"

'He smiled quietly. "Yes," he says, "I believe it would. William was always a bit that way."

'Perhaps I showed what was in my mind.

'"It's all right, Rory," he says. "I have a more cunning way than that of dealing with a fellow like this Don Mackay. Plainly," he says, and him smiling in that d— pleasant way, "plainly this is no place for a chap with that amount of spirit in him. We'll have to ship him abroad. The wild ways of the poaching is in his blood, and most likely he would never knuckle down to us. And that would be a pity, for, in the week or so that I have now been here, I can see how well the people have been trained into a beautiful and complete respect for all the game and other laws that are in it, and you are to be complimented on the – the signal way in which you have done your duty, as also my late lamented brother. Now this fellow – I think I could get a place for him on a certain estate I own in Australia. It's a pretty tough job of adventure, and would, I feel sure, just about suit his case. And if we got rid of him, I don't think there'd be such another spirit left in the place to destroy your night's sleep, Rory, eh! Whereas, if we prosecute, we might have the satisfaction of seeing him pay out a pound or two, but sure enough we'd never stop him. He'd always be a thorn in our flesh."'

Which, as an argument, had proved overwhelming. Rory had not had a word. He glared on his two henchmen now without a word. Then suddenly he spun on his heel and walked into the gloom of the night, seeing only the unfathomable expression in the eyes of the new laird.

# The Man Who Came Back

(STUDY FOR A ONE-ACT PLAY)

*Scots Magazine, 1928*

Granny Cattanach sat on her stiff armchair to the right of the great flat hearth, her soft eyes on the peats. The stone-flagged floor of the kitchen echoed dully the restless footsteps of her grandson Iain, who kept walking about without any mind, as though he were in a cage. In the stillness of the figure by the fire was a listening quality and in the softness of the eye intuition glimmered.

Gently her voice came, kindly, and she did not look up:

'Are you tired, Iain?'

'Tired?' He paused. 'Tired? Oh no!' His voice was amused at the idea; his mouth twisted.

'You had a long day on the hills – a trying day. When you're too tired you just can't rest. You shouldn't have dressed yourself. You should just have gone to your bed.'

He laughed shortly.

'Oh, I'm not tired. It was fine on the hills in the morning – when the sun broke.'

'You'll be getting into it now.'

'A bit, Granny.' He sat down. 'Yes.'

'You're sure you're – you're –' As she hesitated he tilted himself back in his chair and stretched his arms.

'Och, och!' he said, expanding his chest.

Reflectively she stared into the fire. 'Ay ay,' she sighed.

Iain settled down on his chair and stared into the fire, too.

Presently she asked quietly:

'Where's your father?'

'He's out-by somewhere, I think.'

Then at last she looked up at him, her eyes melting with tenderness.

'You're sure you're not – taking long, laddie?'

'Taking long! ' He laughed. 'What would I be longing for?'

There was a reflective moment before she said, turning away to the fire:

'When I was your age I was for a year in service in Edinburgh. It's a lightsome life in the towns yonder.'

'Oh, it's lightsome enough.'

'Yes. And when you are in the towns the hills are in your mind and the old home places, and you see the little crofts and the sheep farms and the Grampian hills, and you say to yourself, *The Grampian Mountains*. Beautiful it sounds. But when you come back – when you come back – after a little –' She hesitated again.

He stretched himself restlessly.

'When you came back,' he repeated, and interrupted himself with a half yawn.

'Ay, it's when you come back,' she murmured.

'So you found it lonely when you came back?'

'No – not lonely. It's not that.'

His eyes narrowed a moment on her averted face.

'No?' he echoed, pleasantly.

'No, it's not the loneliness.'

'What then? The people?'

'No, it's not the people?'

'What was it then, Granny?' And he smiled.

'I don't know,' she said.

'Who would have thought, now, that you looked back on your city life with regrets and longing!'

'I didn't.'

'But –'

'I loved being at home again. The hills and the people and everything. It was good.'

'But – you said –'

She turned her eyes on him and their kindliness penetrated.

'But maybe I can understand a little, for all that.'

'Understand, eh?' he repeated at random, because he could

not hold her eyes.

Gently, persuasively came her voice:

'Don't bother yourself about me, Iain. I'm just your granny and an old, old woman.'

'Bother myself! How do you mean?' He smiled.

She sighed. There was a pause.

'Was your father with you last night?'

'Yes. We took the sheep round by Benglass and we slept in the Tulchan bothy.'

'Were you comfortable and did you sleep?'

'I slept like a stone.'

'That was good.' After a moment she added, 'Your father would sleep well, too, I'm sure.'

'I think so, Granny,' His tone went dry, 'He didn't say.'

'No, he wouldn't. He's not in the habit of saying much at any time, Iain. It was never his way.'

'No, he was never exactly talkative.'

'No, but that doesn't mean – that doesn't mean –'

'That doesn't mean that he doesn't think. I know, Granny – I've heard him at the thinking.'

She tried to search his mood, but he tilted back his chair, the amused flick on his face.

Resignedly she turned to the fire. 'Ay, ay.' She looked up again. 'And what –? ' She paused, her glimmering eyes waiting.

'What did I hear him thinking ?' He got up and stretched himself, half-yawned as he turned his back on the fire. Her question was interesting. 'I'll tell you what I heard him thinking. He was saying to himself – no, that's wrong. He didn't need to say it to himself. A deep conviction doesn't even need internal language.' The thought seemed worth a pause – through which came her gentle tones:

'Maybe you don't understand your father, Iain.'

'Well, now, I wonder, Granny!' he speculated. 'I didn't understand him when I was a boy at school certainly. I knew of course what he spent keeping me in lodgings when I went to the Higher Grade at Kingussie – and afterwards in Glasgow, too, when I went to Mr Black's office to learn the law. The law

here to us means a fine factor's job at least, and a factor is a
high and mighty man. Mr Black, for instance. Now there is
something in the visits of Mr Black to the offices of the estate
here that I can see appealed to my father – not, of course, that
he would ever show anything of the sort! Hardly! There is a
pride about my father, Granny! It is a pride common to all the
finer, silent natures about whose outlook there is a certain
grand unquestioning simplicity. But it is secretive – so very
secretive. Even had I by some marvellous chance jumped right
into Mr Black's shoes, the pride would have shown less than
ever – and most certainly there would have been no word of
praise. No, "Well done, my son!" and a kissing on both
cheeks, for example!' He chuckled softly and took a stride or
two.

'Iain.' Her tone was bright with pain. 'Surely you're not at
your own father!'

'*At* him, Granny? Surely not! I'm *of* him enough to feel a
sort of pride in his pride, in spite of everything. In spite of
everything, and though I know how silly –' He checked
himself in a humoured sniff.

'Silly – silly –' she whispered.

'No, not father that's silly, my dear Granny – he could not
be your son and be silly. It's his attitude. You see, I was *in* Mr
Black's office. I have a certain amount of what is called inside
knowledge of what a lawyer's job can be. But I won't say what
I think of lawyers and their job, Granny. Never mind all that
nasty side of it. Only, I know that Mr Black was hardly fit to
tie the laces on my father's boots. And that's all that matters.'

'Was that really why you left Mr Black?'

'No, not altogether. A man will stand a lot, if he sees an end,
something worth striving –' He did not finish, and after a time
she said quietly:

'And the newspaper office.'

His concentration broke on an ironic note.

'Yes, there was that newspaper office!'

'Well, I don't know,' she murmured in the silence. 'I don't
know … You were always so fond of books. These story
books of yours when you were a little boy … and the poetry.

Your mother – your mother –'

'Yes, she died, Granny, the week after I left for the Higher
Grade. Sometimes I miss her more now than I did then, for I
miss her now with understanding.'

Perceptibly the old body by the fire began to rock, slowly,
eyes on the peat flame.

'Yes,' she whispered, 'yes …'

'But perhaps after all, it's as well. I mean – well, do you
think … what do you think mother would have thought of me
throwing up all my chances, the wonderful chances of getting
on in life – even to the great height of a factor-lawyer –
throwing them up and coming back here – to be a shepherd to
my own father?'

There was no response.

'Come on, Granny! What would she have thought?'

'You know she would have stood up for you.'

'Yes, yes. But what would she have thought – in her heart?'

'Ah – in her heart – her heart –'

'Come on, Granny! Don't be mournful about it.'

The body leant a little more to the fire.

'So it is in your heart too, Granny!' He laughed. 'You see it
is! It would have been in hers, too – no matter how deep she
buried it. I would be – I am – the failure come home. Do you
think I don't know it? The folk look at me, and they think and
nod to one another behind my back. "Yes, poor fellow, he
didn't make much headway – with all his chances.… No, it's
not that easy, with all the schooling and ability that's in it
nowadays.… He'll be feeling it likely.…" You think I don't
see? Ah, yes, Granny, I see all right. I am the one unpardonable
sin – the man who came back to the land.' He laughed. 'Back
to the land– eh, Granny! You know, that's why the lawyers
who are the great politicians – that's why they have to stay in
their big houses in the great cities – so that it will be handy for
them to shout Back to the Land. And sometimes they come
back themselves – for the shooting in the autumn. And they
get refreshed after that and shout harder than ever. And the
fine words they have for it! A nation, they shout, has always
drawn its greatness from the soil. The depopulation of our

rural areas and the over-population of our towns is the beginning of the end of our national greatness, the first fly in the Imperial ointment –' He stopped abruptly and took down the violin from the wall by the mantelpiece. Slowly he tuned it, plucking at the strings with a firm thumb. But when the fifths ran perfectly under the thumb, he paused, shrugged, and hung the violin up again.

Dumbly she looked up at him a moment.

'Won't you have a tune to yourself, Iain?'

'Ach, I'm off it!' He sat down and produced his smile. 'Well, Granny,' he said pleasantly, 'so you see I know what father thinks.'

'I don't know,' she answered tonelessly.

'Ay, you know fine. To my father I am his son who has failed. That gets him. That's bitter. But he won't mention it. Oh, no – any more than he would have mentioned my success. The pride, Granny – the pride of the hills ... like a sheathed sword.'

'I don't know.'

'Ay, you know fine,' he laughed. 'Oh, fine that!'

There was a pause, until at last she lifted her head and forced her words bravely:

'Then why – why did you – come back?'

'At last, Granny, eh?'

'Why – why, Iain?'

He returned her look, his expression steadying, his inner thought rising to the verge of utterance, when the kitchen door opened and Mary, the hired girl, came in. Iain turned round in his chair pleasantly.

'Well, Mary, is that you?'

'Yes,' said Mary; but she did not look at him, and a small flame gathered in her face as she turned to the dresser. She lifted a candlestick and paused a moment looking about the dresser, then turned to the fire.

'A light, is it?' he asked.

'Yes,' she said. She picked up a scrap of paper. 'This will do.' She lit the candle.

'It's milking time,' said Granny Cattanach quietly.

'Yes,' said Mary, 'I'll put this candle in the lantern.'

Iain stirred and asked naturally:

'Can I help you?'

'Oh no, thanks,' replied Mary, quickly. 'I'll manage.' Her dark lashes swept her dark eyes but could not hide their gleam.

'Did you see the master, Mary?'

'I saw him on the edge of the darkening with Rob o' Kinbreac,' said Mary to her. 'I think Andrew McIntosh's cow had some sort of turn. They went that way.'

'I hope it's not much,' said Granny Cattanach.

'I don't think so.' Mary hesitated a moment, eyes to the door. But before she had passed out Iain was staring reflectively into the fire, her advent having apparently touched him in no way. As on a sudden thought, he threw a quick glance at the wag-at-th'-wa'. Silence.

Granny Cattanach stirred reflectively.

'Yes ... yes ...'

'Ay ay,' stirred Iain, his tone easy.

But Granny Cattanach was groping back to the interrupted mood.

'Ah, well ...'

Iain tilted his chair back and stretched himself, baffling her. 'Och och.'

'So – so that was it?'

'Ah, well, Granny, that's the way of things.' He got up again – and became aware of his own restlessness. She looked at him.

'That's your book there on the corner of the mantelpiece.'

'Oh yes, the book.' He lifted the book, looked at it, laid it down again. He stuck his hands in his pockets and whistled a note or two of no tune.'

'Iain!' she appealed.

'Ay ay, Granny.' He smiled. 'I'm off the books, too. I'm sort of off everything tonight, eh.'

'Oh, Iain, Iain!'

'Uhm.'

'You have your own pride and it as strong as your father's and your heart is as hidden. Have you ever told him why you came back? Have you? Have you?'

He was considering her words, eyelids flickering half ironi-
cally, when voices were heard without. The door opened and
his father ushered in Rob Grant of Kinbreac and Andrew
M<sup>c</sup>Intosh.

'Come away! Come away in!' cried Granny Cattanach
hospitably.

Rob Grant came first, his round lined face and small
twinkling eyes nodding a greeting.

'Well, Mistress, how are you to-night?'

'Fine! Fine! Take a chair!'

Iain got up.

'Don't move,' said Rob. 'I'll sit here opposite your Granny.'

Andrew M<sup>c</sup>Intosh's loose-jointed, big-boned body came up
to Iain.

'Ay Iain, boy, and how's the shepherding?'

'Oh, not so bad, man; not so bad!'

'You'll be getting seasoned like the rest of us now, I'll
wager!'

'What else!'

'How's the dog doing?'

'She stayed last night without showing any signs of wanting
to cut back to you, and she worked like a charm all this
morning.... I can imagine a man being sorry to part with his
dog.'

'Oh, well, you'll not have to part with her, anyway....
Unless, of course, you'll be hungering already for the girls you
left behind you!'

Cattanach had drawn a couple of chairs towards the fire
and now as he sat down there came a subtly expressionless
'Hm!' from his nostrils. But his strong reticent face gave no
sign.

'Well, there are the girls, to be sure!' laughed Iain, subtly
reacting.

'Oh, the weemun, the weemun!' gloated Rob pawkily.

With a sweet gentle smile on her thin worn face, Granny
Cattanach smoothed her dark apron over and over.

'Oh, there are great ones yonder by all accounts!' reckoned

Andrew, in his big voice.

'Wheesht!' said Iain.

Rob eyed him.

'Eh? Oh, the weemun!' He laughed, his small eyes twinkling meaningfully.

'Man, Iain, wouldn't Rob be the sight now walking down yon streets and her with all her feathers and paint and gew-gaws on her! Boys-a-boys, there would be a cut on him; and she would have the swish on her silks like the rain on the bracken.' And Andrew laughed throatily

'Poor Andrew's getting a bit-auld-fashioned, Granny, eh?' appealed Rob. 'They would know he came from the heather when he would be thinking of a dress long enough to have a swish to it!'

'Oh, he may not be so old-fashioned as all that, if every-thing we hear is true!' returned Granny, aware of her son's unyielding quietude as he slowly began to fill his pipe, eyes on the fire.

'You think he'll be pretending?' Rob took her up. 'Indeed, I have heard things myself, but I'll no' just say!'

'Do you see how he would seduce me?' asked Andrew; and as Iain laughed, added, 'Well, if that's not the word it's one just like it,' and he rubbed his crown facetiously.

'You'll have to take a trip to Glasgow, Rob, so that you could explain to Andrew the proper way to go about it,' suggested Iain.

'Maybe, maybe,' returned Andrew. 'But who would take Rob's hand down the streets? A fine middle-aged bachelor like him now, with a house waiting!'

'Leave that to me,' offered Iain. 'I'll show him the way to Sauchiehall Street and all the painted ladies.'

Cattanach stirred on his chair and spat deliberately into the fire. Granny threw him a quick look.

'That's you!' said Andrew. 'I wouldn't risk him alone – but if you would go with him....'

'Don't worry!' came Iain's clear laughing voice; 'I'll be there before him.' And it was suddenly as though all the kitchen heard it and tried to steal a look at him – all, that is, except the eyes of his father – without, however, disturbing the delicacy of the slow, half-conventional humour of the occasion.

'It might be safer indeed,' smiled Andrew at once, 'if you did go with him!'

'Well, if he could make up his mind quick enough, he might catch Donald the carter with me tonight yet. It hasn't struck nine.' He threw a glance at the wag-at-th'-wa'. They all threw a glance at it – except his father, who was smoking quietly, gaze on the fire. Then their eyes returned surreptitiously to Iain's face. Andrew felt reassured by the pleasant humour he saw there.

'I'm afraid that might just be a bit too quick for Rob!' he reckoned.

'You'd wonder, too, man, Andrew, what the swish might do!' hinted Rob.

'Oh, no doubt! It would be a change from the swish of the bracken in the Vrachkin!'

'Ay, a change!' put in Iain, searchingly.

'And maybe we'd never see him back at all,' doubted Andrew. 'The sheep and the croft would be a bit too slow for him after yon!'

'You think he wouldn't be disturbed, now, by the memories of the glen?' searched Iain. 'On a hot summer day, say, you think he wouldn't be hearing the swish of the scythe through that other swish on the hot pavements? He wouldn't be wishing himself among the long quiet hours on the hill, or spending a night at the bothy when the cattle are up at the summer grazings? You don't think he would long for the stars when the flaring globes of Sauchiehall Street would be dazing his eyes, nor for the sound of the Vrachkin burn on a still night, when the giggle of the painted lips was in his ears? Uh?'

'Well – what?' Andrew laughed uncertainly.

With his pleasant smile, Iain proceeded:

'And you don't think he would be saying to himself that there was a sickness on him and that Glasgow was choking him in the throat, that it was dimming his eyes so that he could hardly see Corrievrachkin at all, so far away it looked, like the memory of a lovely thing that was dead? Uh?' Through the smile the eyes narrowed on Andrew and a flick of irony curled the lips. 'You don't think he would say to himself, "By heavens, now, I am tired of this, of all the heat and the cackle and the lies and the money-grabbing and the paint and the whole rotten rickmatick; by heavens, but my soul is sick of it and it's up I'll get and go back to the land of my fathers, where peace is, and men stop to look at the sky without getting run down or run in." Do you think he would say, "Corrievrachkin, Corrievrachkin – the sound of you in my ears is like the sound of the word of the Lord; ye shall be my tabernacle before the eternities and I will lie on my back on your altar and listen to the honey bees and smell the incense of the heather and not give a damn for the false gods anymore," – uh?'

'Och och!' twisted Andrew, trying to look nowhere!

'You bet he would have more sense!' laughed Iain. 'He would know. He would know.'

'What would I know?' asked Rob, his small eyes watching Iain.

Iain turned to him.

'You would know that once having set out to make your way, to get on in the great world, there was no longer anything but the one thing.'

'What?'

'There was no turning back.'

'Oh,' said Rob, watching him narrowly.

'Yes,' nodded Iain into Rob's watching eyes. 'To go away to the towns and to come back with a collar on to show yourself to the glen folk for a day or two – on holiday! – that is not merely to fulfil yourself, Rob, but to achieve the higher aims of destiny before the eyes of your own kinsfolk. And the mothers will say to their bare-legged sons, "Do you see Robert Grant there walking about like a gentleman? It'll be the bonny day before ever you walk about like that! ..." But, Rob, if you had set off with your father's good money spent on your schooling and your learning, set off in great style to occupy higher spheres – and after a few years had come back – to stay ... *to stay*, Rob ... back for good ... what would they say then? What?' His quiet laugh probed. 'Ay, I see you know what they

would say. And even in the glens beyond the hills a mother
would hit out at her son with "Ah, ye little good-for-nothing,
you'll be just another Robbie Grant!" In a word, Rob, you
would be the unpardonable sin – the man who came back to
Corrievrachkin.'

Rob kept looking, his small acute eyes trying to penetrate
the hidden meanings. Andrew, pushing his chair back noisily,
made an effort at a natural smile, but, glimpsing Granny
Cattanach's suspiciously glistening eyes, became more uncomfortable than ever. Cattanach himself smoked on imper-
turbably. Time drew out to a thin tension, suddenly smashed
by the first harsh metallic stroke of the clock striking the hour.
One, two ... the inner works whirring in a wild humour, cut
off by the ninth stroke.

Iain straightened himself; buttoned his jacket.

'But, Rob,' and he smiled sardonically into the watching
eyes, 'when you found that what you came back for, what you
were hungry for, was – was ... and you went away for the
second time ... then you would never come back, *cha till e
tuille,* nevermore.' He walked with sauntering naturalness to
the door. As he opened it, he turned and looked at his granny,
let his eyes rest a moment on his father, then went out.

Andrew broke the silence.

'Well, it's time I ...' He craned exaggeratedly at the clock.

Cattanach turned to him with quiet hospitality.

'Sit down, Andrew.'

'Oh – I think –'

Cattanach looked at the clock.

'It's just struck nine. You don't need to give her the hot
bran-mash till the half hour. Sit down, man.'

Andrew sat down and cleared his throat as though he were
trying to clear the kitchen. Rob was now studying the fire and
suddenly said, 'Ay,' hanging to the vowel sound thoughtfully.

'Yes, man,' twisted Andrew; 'yes –'

'It has the appearance of making a good morning,' said
Cattanach.

'Oh, I think so,' agreed Andrew readily; 'every indication. I
was just –' Outside a dog howled, and the mournful sound

bayed about the wide kitchen. Through a tense listening Rob raised his head and looked queerly at Andrew.

'That's the dog you gave him.'

'Is it? Yes, ay, she'll be a little strange yet.' Andrew fumbled in his pockets. Granny gave a single quiet sob.

'She worked well to-day,' said Cattanach evenly. 'There are the makings of a good dog in her.'

'Yes. She ought to be. She ought to be.' Andrew found his pipe and hung on to it.

'Ay,' said Rob to the fire.

'The mother was that bitch of Achnahine's, wasn't she?' remembered Cattanach.

'Yes, yes. I got her from him,' replied Andrew. 'It was my own dog, Carlo – Carlo – you know Carlo …'

Cattanach turned a level look at him.

'Of course I know Carlo.'

'Of course! I knew you did … every day …' He smiled hurriedly.

'Ay,' sucked in Rob.

Into the silence came a sound of quick footsteps from without. The door swung open and Mary entered, her face pale and strained with emotion. She was taken aback at the men in the kitchen and stiffened against the door, breath held.

'Mary, what is it?' came Granny's whisper.

'Nothing,' gulped the hired girl.

'Mary!'

Cattanach turned slowly round and looked at her.

'He passed me – he was going down the glen – away –'

'Did he – say –' managed Granny.

'He did not see me. He was – he was – crying.' Her voice broke on a sob and she hurriedly went out, banging the door shut behind her. The men's faces remained on the door, but Granny's eyes were already on the fire, her body slowly rocking.

# The Storm

*Scots Magazine, 1935*

Always when the darkness of storm deepens in the sky there is born the uneasy fear that some boat may have been caught beyond the bar. And now it was certain that the *White Rose* had not returned.

A small undecked boat used mostly for the winter line fishing, she was skippered by old Sans, one of the finest fishermen on the coast, with Willie, his son, and Gordon, his nephew, for crew. Willie and Gordon being in their twenties were but lads under the dominion of Sans, who was quiet and orderly in his ways, bred to the sea, weather tough, and nearly seventy.

To those converging on the harbour, it was somehow astonishing that it should be Sans who had not returned. The uneasiness steadily grew. The tide had only just started making, and on the shallows of the bar the waves were already breaking as on a reef. Indeed the heavy movement of the sea was so much greater than the wind as yet warranted, that the whole weather outlook was ugly. The sky was growing a dirty black. The heaving water was dirty-looking, too, all its blue-green transparency utterly gone; and the churning foam was an unearthly white. The evil principle of death in the sea could be seen coming actively to life.

Thinking of Sans, several of the watchers smiled, as if half in wonder what he could be up to; though on that rock-bound coast manifestly a fisherman could not be up to anything much other than catching fish and making straight for harbour.

It was neither the place nor the time for Sans to be provoked into argument over fishing politics. He had a more active force than the Government to contend with now! Here was the very ironic moment to prove his notion that the individual fisherman was as strong and self-reliant as he had ever been and the Government as futile to assist! Couldn't be bettered! Not that Sans wanted the Government to assist him. He wanted no one's assistance. But it was his simple belief that if the fisherman's job was to catch fish, it was the Government's job to arrange about foreign markets. And in Sans' opinion the Government had made a hash of their job.

Not that he spoke readily of these things, for the true rhythm and power of the sea were in him, and far in the back of his mind was a silent contempt for all professional talkers.

But this political oddity of his was just sufficient to relieve or at least to temper the fear of the moment. So younger men joked, wondering how Sans was getting on in his present little argument with the sea, and others smiled, their eyeballs shining as the salted wind stung them to tears.

But a few of the older women had the mournful tremor in their voices. The underlying anxiety was pushing up in arrowy spouts here and there. Some of the more active men were now seen far out on the point to the left, leaning against the wind. From the rocks below them clouds of spume rose in a burst, hung suspended, and slowly fell back. Clearly excitement of some kind was already grouping them round a figure with a spyglass. Was something being seen? For the glass passed from one to another, to be levelled always in the same direction.

In a very short time everyone knew that a small-boat was lying in the shelter of the distant Head.

This Head was a promontory of sheer precipice that ran far out into the sea, and in the grey storm haze, with the waves smashing on its point, it looked forbidding as doom. Nor could the glass help the naked eye much, because of the haze. But that a small-boat was, for the time being, finding some shelter on the near side of that dark rock face was certain; and that it could not be any boat but Sans' was accepted by all as equally certain. A few indeed asserted that they could see three figures in the boat, and one young man, athletic and keen-eyed, went the length of maintaining that he could see Sans fishing. That was too much of a joke! But the young fellow, Jeck, insisted. Had he not been out with Sans? He knew exactly where Sans always sat and how, when he was feeling for a strike, his whiskered chin tilted up a bit as if he were listening.

Too much altogether, that!

'You'll see him spitting next.' They rocked with laughter in their relief; they teased Jeck, but could not make him angry. Jauntily he hitched himself up, his blue eyes flashing. When he looked through the spyglass again, a lad shot a sly spittle in front of the lens.

But the older men were puzzled. The position was more than hazardous. Sans had nowhere to run to, and the wind had to shift round only a point or two for his temporary shelter to become more dangerous than any other spot on that coast. Was Sans expecting that when they had seen him they would launch the lifeboat? Yet he had hoisted no signals. He might not like to do that, leaving the position to their wisdom. He was an independent old fellow who would put up his own desperate fight rather than beg for their help. 'If they cannot see I'm in danger, it's little good telling them,' they could imagine his saying quietly. And they all felt there was some truth in that. For no one concerned was it the moment to make a fuss. Then the harbourmaster said: 'One thing is quite clear: he could never live in that sea now if he tried to come home himself. And it's worse it's getting.'

This plain statement of fact relieved their minds, for it made their duty clear. Another man said: 'He's lying there until the tide makes enough for him to try the bar. It's his only chance, and, as you say, not much of a chance at that.'

But half tide would not be for another couple of hours, and the lifeboat herself must, on returning, make the harbour. There was no hurry, yet they might as well get the crew together, have things shipshape, and in a little while put to sea, so that old Sans need not begin any desperate venture under the delusion that he had not been seen.

Nearly all the inhabitants of that place lined the shore as the lifeboat was launched and took the seas head-on. They were proud of their lifeboat, and as she fell with a smashing sound on the waters, rose and dipped out of sight, a queer drawn joy gripped their hearts. An old woman wept; a daring boy here and there hit another in the ribs to save himself from any unmanly expression of his excitement.

The course of the lifeboat was followed eagerly.'She's making heavy weather of it. Ay, a dirty sea.' The wind bore the high words away. Eyes shone with a strange wild humour. For what might have been tragedy was clearly being made safe; the demon in the sea was to be defeated, let him thunder as he liked; and all the sport of defeating him remained yet to be seen.

'Isn't she looking little already? She's being tossed like a cork, isn't she, Dad?' cried one little boy.

'Would you like to be one of the crew on the lifeboat, Ian?' asked a smiling young woman beside him.

'I would,' said Ian, then swung himself on his father's hand, ashamed of his thought having been seen. The young woman half-tickled, half-fondled him.

'Stop it!' cried Ian, 'or I'll give you a kick.'

'Oh, Ian!'

He wriggled from his father's hand and ran away.

'She's making in for them now,' muttered Jeck's mouth beneath the glass.

'We can see that ourselves! Is Sans still fishing?'

'Yes.'

Sceptical laughter shook them.

'Is he getting anything?' asked a mock innocent voice.

'I – think so,' said Jeck. 'He's bending over now – he must have landed one.'

'What are you seeing now?'

Without lowering the glass or opening his left eye, Jeck spat expertly on the finger in front of the lens.

'Steady, boys,' said a grey-haired man. 'Can you see them now, Jeck?'

'Yes. They're standing in to come up alongside... They've

put her about. I can't see them very clearly... They're on this side of Sans, now ... I can't see Sans' boat.'

The white of the lifeboat was visible enough to keen eyes.

'It'll be quieter there than we think. Sans would have been close in. They'll be taking them on board.'

'I don't know what they're doing,' said Jeck. 'They seem to be doing nothing.'

'Oh, to blazes, give me that glass!' cried an impatient voice.

'Shut up!' said Jeck, with explosive fierceness. After all, his father was skipper of the lifeboat.

'What now, Jeck?' asked the grey-haired man quietly.

Jeck was silent.

'I see her, I think ... they're not alongside.' Jeck spoke a trifle doubtfully. 'Yes – I think – ' Then his voice rose sharply. 'I see her – not alongside.'

'Of course!' shouted the impatient voice. 'When they take them aboard they'll cast her off and tow her astern. What did you think?'

'She's not astern,' said Jeck, speaking to himself. 'They're still aboard her.'

'Steady, Jeck,' said the old man.

'They're still aboard her. Sans is standing up. He's doing something ... the sail.'

'Don't be a fool!'

'Yes, there she is. The sail. They're going to sail her. They're standing out.'

This was sheer madness. But eyes could now see something. Then a man cried in a great voice: 'By God, Sans is sailing her!'

Each body quivered coldly.

What in the name of the seven seas could have happened? Here was something beyond all reason or understanding.

Jeck lowered the glass. 'All three of them are aboard.' His face was white, his hands restless.

Silence fell on them there on the sea-point, then flowed inward toward the harbour wall in a cold invisible wave.

Sailing her – into that!

Lord God of the oceans!

Old faces drooped as if blinded. Bodies quivered back.

Back from the shock of engulfing waters, that thundered there on the bar. Thundered and boiled. The boats in the walled basin went creaking and moaning on their ropes as the lifting tide got them.

And Sans was such a sane fellow, such a quiet old man; independent and with plenty of sea pride in him, but never boastful, never foolish. What could have gone wrong ? It could not be fear for his boat ? No, they would tow his boat. They could try, anyhow, and if she filled they could cut her adrift. Sans might risk his own life for a boat, the times being what they were, but he would hardly risk the lives of the other two. It was not to save the boat...

And she was making headway. Her dark peak of sail, like a shark's fin, rose into sight and disappeared, cut the surface again and was lost. Behind her swung the lifeboat, playing the same desperate game of hide-and-seek.

No word was spoken now on the sea-point. Jeck's limber body, taut as a quivering mast, took the rock-roar and the whistling wind, and the outward surge of his spirit could have sailed the earth itself to their rescue.

When the dark fin disappeared, life hung in sickening suspense. It appeared again. But only for a moment, and it was gone ... down into the depths ... down ... down under? ... There! there it is!

But the shout was voiceless, for even as they looked, the sail had vanished once more.

Men's games of speed-racing or bull-fighting are staged performances in danger, and the thrill is for nerves seeking the old elemental encounter. Nerves artificially stimulated to savour the ancient blood excitement.

There was no artificial stimulation here. No blood lust in this for Sans or his spectators, no throttling down of that titanic power, no piercing of its bloodless shoulders with any quivering spear. Nature had staged this show after her immemorial fashion.

The hard stress eased a little from the breasts of men, as they saw Sans holding his own in the encounter. His sail kept appearing and reappearing like the mythical fight of the living soul in its escape from the terrifying powers of the inanimate.

There was exaltation in it; but fear, gripping the bowels, continued to squeeze a sickliness into the throat.

Feathers of spume from the rocks were driven into men's faces by the hunting destroying wind – that Sans caught in his triangle of sail to help his escape.

Now the dark hull of his boat could be discerned. At last men began to speak. In their sober voices there was an odd under-ring of admiration, of defiance, of fear.

When Sans would put her about to run for the harbour, when she would swing broadside on, could she survive the desperate moment, could she live?

No one asked that question.

As the moment drew near, silence caught the watchers again.

Now, now. No, not yet. Now – yes! ... there he goes! He's round! By God, he's gone!

No! There he comes! He's coming!

Bow and sail shore clear up on the wave-top, hung a moment, then slid stern first ... ?

There he is! Boys, boys, he's holding to it! Good old Sans! Keep her at it, Sans! Lord, he's doing it, boys!

The excitement became insupportable. The wind drew tears out of staring eyes. Bodies, braced and quivering, began to stamp the earth. Teeth chittered.

And now it was almost laughable to see the lifeboat coming behind that tossing cork of a boat. Like a great cat hunting a mouse; playing a game of their own in the swinging hollows of death.

Dammit, trust old Sans! He knows! What! Sideways, half-stumbling, running a step or two, eyes glistening, the men on the sea-point began to make for the harbour.

Nothing was said of safety, for Sans had yet to cross the bar.

With weather room about him and depth beneath, a man can put up his fight with design. But over the shallows of treachery, the rudder of purpose is useless, and the indomitable mind can be choked by spume.

Well they knew that. And their practised eyes gauged the

depth of water by the way the wave curled over and broke. Already they could see the deepest part of the channel – less than a fathom wide it seemed – where the wave swung solidly on, leaving its extended arms smashing in froth.

Sans was coming dead for it. A few minutes earlier it had not been there.

They could see him clearly now, his right forearm along the tiller, bending forward a little in an easy posture. He never moved nor acknowledged in any way those who crowded the shore. He was coming at speed, too ... Look out, Sans – behind you!

The sea caught him and flung him forward with great velocity – and left him. He had missed it. He was broaching, too. He would be in the shallows.

Sans lay back a little. The *White Rose* had a neat forefoot; it clove and hissed; she kept her seaway. It would have dishonoured her had she lost it then. But she had been through a bit too much for that. Too much!

Look out!

Trim and taut and cleaving ahead, the singing hiss of her slender stem over the treachery of the bar, she caught hold of the last wave and rode it into the middle of the basin.

Old Sans had won through! The pent-up excitement at last found its voice in shouts and laughter.

But old Sans gave no response. When they cried to him down the harbour wall, he did not answer, did not lift his head. He was quietly putting things shipshape, the sail, the gear, leaving a large catch of white fish visible in the well of the boat.

But his son, Willie, looked up with a knowing smile, and silently winked.

They understood in a flash. Sans disliked all this fuss, this public demonstration over nothing! Some fell back a pace under the surge of their half-choked mirth. This was the best joke yet! Elbows dug into ribs, a wild humour shone in glancing eyes. Sans' strong face remained quiet, expressionless, almost gentle!

What in the world had really happened out there?

Ah, here was one of the lifeboat crew, already surrounded
by a knot of folk that rumbled with laughter. Yet the laughter
did not even here really release the gaiety; it only made it
glisten all the more incredibly in the eye.

The lifeboatman was relating how they had borne down on
Sans and found him fishing.

'You were right after all, Jeck!' exclaimed a voice.

Jeck smiled, his clear eyes turned with some embarrassment
towards the group above Sans' boat; the young woman with
the dark, bare head, poised on the very edge of the harbour
wall, was Sans' daughter.

'Fishing away,' explained the lifeboatman, 'with his chin up
a bit – like that – and not seeing us. Just as Jeck's father hailed
him he struck a fine cod, and was so busy hauling it in, he paid
no attention to us at all. By the time that was all over, we were
near enough to spit on them. Then he looked up – and kept
looking with seemingly great astonishment. You would think
we had dropped from the clouds. "What are ye wanting?" he
cried.'

His listeners rocked.

'What are ye wanting?' they mimicked, with grotesque
innocence. Superb!

'Yes, just as if we'd been hunting him for a pipe of tobacco!
Jeck's father cried: "We've come out to take you home. Don't
you see the sea that's in it?"'

'Old Sans looked about him. Then he got slowly to his feet.
The whole Head was roaring like thunder. The *White Rose*
was like a swing under him. With both feet on her, as you
might say, he looked across at us. "What's that?" he cried.
"For fifty years I've taken my boat home without anyone's
help: I'm not likely to start taking yours now!" At that he
turned his shoulder on us and sat down.

'Man, we did not know where the devil we were. Plainly he
was boiling up, though he looked calm enough. One thing was
certain to every one of us: Sans would never accept our help
now. We knew as much by the very set of him. Indeed before
he opened his mouth at all, most of us guessed how the wind
lay. It was extraordinary!

'But our skipper was nettled. Dammit, we were wet from the neck down. And it did make us out to be fools. Though there was a sort of grim humour in it, too. Anyway, whatever we thought, our skipper shouted: "Well, if you want to drown, that's your business. What about your crew?"'

'Willie looked over and winked. Gordon smiled, too. Naturally they wouldn't think of leaving the old man. At that your father, Jeck, as if he had said too much, got more nettled. "Don't be a fool, Sans," he shouted. "You'll never live in that sea. We didn't come out here for fun. Damn you, man, can't you have some sense?"'

'Sans got to his feet again. Oh, boys!'

'What did he say?'

'Hush – there's Sans coming up,' said Jeck.

The old skipper in his dark blue jersey stepped up on to the quay behind the two lads with the herring basket full of white fish.

'Dirty weather, Sans,' remarked one of his grey-bearded friends to him.

'Ay,' said Sans in a mild tone, 'there's a bit of a lift in it outside.'

The eyes of his old friend twinkled.

'Had the lifeboat a good fishing?'

'Not very, I think,' remarked Sans. 'But that will be all right. The Government will give them medals.'

As he walked away home, his dark-haired daughter had the wisdom to make no remark to him at all. She looked all the same as if she were singing with happiness. Jeck was so fascinated watching the departure, that he missed the culminating joke altogether.

A little later he was leaning against the door-post of his home, when he saw the dark girl come along with a burden of fish.

'Is your father in, Jeck?'

'Yes,' he said, 'yes.' His body had all at once grown very active but without direction. He shouted inside: 'Here's Nan!' Then he flushed – and remained outside.

He heard Nan's voice: 'My father sent me along with this fish to you.'

The women's voices were quick and friendly, obviously covering the pause in his father's thought. At last his father was heard in a quiet dry humour: 'That's the second time he's done me this day!'

There was a happy laugh at that.

They would not let Nan go, but she said: 'I'll really have to run.'

Jeck wanted to run too, but the machinery that controlled his body was whirring out of gear.

She had dark eyes as well as dark hair, and her brow was smooth as her cheeks. Her mouth was so expressive that he had to answer it.

'Your father was a bit mad today, wasn't he?' he said, with a foolish laugh of admiration for her father.

The dark eyes flashed their devilment.

'He had courage, anyway!' she answered. The look lingered, the mouth withdrawing to one side in mockery.

But she was in a hurry. She ran. He heard her chuckle of delicious laughter. Then his legs started carrying him away nowhere at a great rate. The guilt of the awkward fool was so heavy upon him that it fancied the houses had found him out and were watching and grinning.

# The Boat: Being the Story of a True Happening

*Scots Magazine, 1937*

The mouth of the Ullie was grey with people when at last the four young men got the boat all ready to shove off. For the first time since the folk had been burned out of their holdings far back in Strach Ullie or Kildonan, a gust of the old communal mirth caught them up. Nor was the mirth the less vocal because of the anxiety behind it. This was a desperate venture and God alone knew what might come out of it. The alternatives at least were simple: food or disaster. Hugh Sutherland, a broad-shouldered, powerful, dark fellow in his middle twenties, was the moving spirit of the crew. There was pride in the way he lurched over the stones of the beach and countered every sally with a wit that brought colour to his own cheeks and laughter to all.

None of the four of them knew anything about the sea or about boats. But Hugh was not going to sit down on a barren beach and starve if he could help it.

'They can't burn us off the sea anyway!' he cried.

True for Hugh! There was game in him. His young wife's cheeks were whipped with colour and her eyes very bright. When she heard an old woman snuffling and whining in a half-keen, she sunk her fingers in her friend's arm. The old fool!

For Hugh and his three friends were already committed deeply to this new venture. To buy the old tub of a boat and fit her out complete with net and lines, they had had to sell some of their cattle; but Hugh got over that by saying that the beasts would have died in any case on the rocky barren sea-face of grazing ground allotted to them.

And perhaps there was truth in that, too.

'It's the sea or nothing, so far as I can see,' was the way he had summed the matter up. 'If you go under with the sea – well, you go right under, and that's something.'

The defiant, jaunty air was about him today more than ever. As he caught the gunnel, a wave creamed up to his knees, and he pulled his feet out as if he had been stung. But he met the laugh good-naturedly. 'That's the baptism!' he cried.

They were delighted with him, for he put hope into them. It was a fine afternoon, with an air of wind off the land. The sea was blue-green and bright and broke in lazy wavelets along the shore. There were tried weather prophets among the older men, and from the appearance of the sky and the way the wind had been working round, they were unanimous in forecasting a fine night.

No harm would come to the boys from the weather, and if they were careful not to fall overboard, then they should return all right, whether they got fish or not. At least there was no landlord or bailiff or other human enemy to interfere with them on the sea! They had that certainty, whatever else!

The four lads eased the boat off until only her nose was on the shingle.

'In with you!' said Hugh.

When the three had clambered aboard, Hugh pushed off and jumped, landing neatly in the bows.

'Good for you, Hugh!' piped young voices from the water's edge. But Hugh was too concerned now with getting the oars working properly to let them have one back.

'Hold your oar in, Ian,' he whispered, and began to pull with all his strength. They had had some practice with the oars bringing the boat up from Golspie. The old man from whom they had bought her had told them all they knew about seafaring. And if Hugh's head wasn't crammed with odd facts, it wasn't from lack of asking questions.

With Ian holding water, Hugh soon had the bow swinging round to sea. 'Pull, Ian!' But Hugh himself was pulling so hard that, what with the swing he had given the boat, her bow was almost pointing inshore again before Ian could get any way on. Hugh now held water, exasperated because they were not making a good start. When the bow began to come round once more, he dug his oar in fiercely. 'Keep her like that!' he cried and gave way with all his force.

Ian, a slim figure of about Hugh's own age, lay on his oar as on his life. At the pull back his body was levered off the seat and writhed like an eel. He had not Hugh's bull-shoulders, but he had all Hugh's pride, and would sooner that his sinews cracked than that his tongue cried halt. But the boat was now gathering way, and Ronnie at the tiller began to feel the kick of Hugh's oar. Ronnie was the oldest by a couple of years and the excitement in him merely made his lean, sallow face sallower than usual. His eyes gleamed with the knowledge that he was guiding Hugh's wild strength and sending the boat straight on her course. 'You're doing great!' he said in a low voice. The two oars described a high half circle, hit the water, and dug in. 'Boys, we're making a good show!'

The chortling pleasure in Ronnie's voice was a great encouragement. Hugh's face got red and congested. Ian was all whipcord. Torquil, who was no more than eighteen, could hardly sit still beside Ronnie. His was the only fair head in that small open boat, and the blue eyes were glancing like the sea water.

When they had gone about half a cable from the shore, a little silence fell upon the watching crowd. There was suddenly something very affecting in the sight of the boat leaving them. It was not a farewell, because the boys would be back in the morning. And yet it was more like a farewell than anything they had known – except the leave-taking of the men who had been shipped to America and whom they need never hope to see again in this life. But that had had all the air of fatality. This was not fatal. Yet, behold! there they were, of themselves, adventuring into the unknown, prepared to live through the darkness of night on the wastes of this new and treacherous element, in the hope of bringing back food to the hungry. Here and there an unconscious muttering rose up as a prayer to God to look after them. Many more than Hugh's wife would watch through the night until the grey of the dawn showed up the boat again. Here surely was the new hope, for behind all God was good. Most of the younger folk were full of a hectic excitement, and for the first time since they had been driven from their ancient homes to make room for sheep, there came quickeningly amongst them a flickering of the old gaiety of the ceilidh-house.

When the boat had gone some way from the beach, Ronnie said: 'Ease up, boys, or you'll pull your guts out.'

'No, no; not yet,' said Hugh. 'Keep her going, Ian.'

'I'll keep her going till I burst,' said Ian.

'Good for you!' cried Ronnie. 'Torquil and I will then have a turn and we'll show you a thing or two. Boys, we're doing fine, and it's a grand night.'

Their hearts swelled up with pleasure and courage. It would take something to stop them now!

Soon the shore was remote from them and the folk looked small and wandered about like little calves. They changed places with such care that the boat hardly rocked at all. Hugh wiped the sweat out of his eyes and Ian separated his shoulders from his shirt. As they settled down again and looked about them, they realised not only that they were cut away from the excitement of the beach but were at last by themselves on the breast of the ocean.

The ocean was alive under them in a way that they dared not think about. At every stroke the depth was increasing. Anything falling overboard now would go down, down, until one could choke thinking about it. So they did not think about it. But they felt it. They felt it as a man with no head for heights can feel himself falling before he has quite come to the edge of the cliff. The sea rose up under them, left them, and passed on.

'There's no hurry, boys,' said Hugh from the tiller. 'I'll be keeping my eyes open now for the signs.'

The old Golspie man had named certain landmarks that he himself always opened out or got in line, but Hugh could make nothing of them now, though he talked confidently enough, saying: 'There's Brora,' or 'That's Tarbat Ness,' or 'That – that must be Berriedale Head.' For he had a sanguine nature and liked being in charge of things.

When the beach seemed very remote from them, Hugh thought they might take a rest and have a try with one of the two lines. 'If you don't find them in one place you'll find them in another,' he said, repeating the Golspie man.

From the pail of boiled limpets, he took four and gouged out the baits with his thumb. He fixed two on each hook, the hard leathery surfaces to the inside. 'That's the way it's done,' he explained cheerfully, and dropped the hooks and heavy sinker overboard.

As yard after yard of line went out, they got a new way of realising the sea's depth. 'You'd almost be drowned if you fell in!' said Hugh. They grew silent. At last the line went slack. 'When you get bottom, you lift it up a yard or two, like that, and then work it up and down.' The three of them watched him.

They watched him until his mouth fell open. 'I think I've got something!' he gulped. He pulled, but the line would not come up. 'It comes a little way, and then pulls back. It must be a whale!' What if it was a whale!

The forked birch stick round which the line was wound was nearly pulled out of Hugh's hands. He had to let out more line. A little more. Leviathan was moving away from under them!

Their hearts went across them. The boat rose on the heave; water slapped her weather side so smartly that they turned their heads.

Suddenly Ronnie cried: 'It's the boat that's drifting!'

Their voices rose shrilly. Ian and Ronnie struggled with the oars. In getting her head into the wind, which was stronger here than it had been under the shelter of the land, they caused her to lurch, and Hugh, tumbling backwards, broke the strain in the line. On his knees again, he began hauling in rapidly. The hooks, the stiff wire, and the sinker were gone.

Hugh stared at the bare end of the line a long time. Was there going to be no luck with them? Slowly he wound the line on to the stick.

'We'll have to go farther out,' he said.

Ian and Ronnie took the oars. Torquil was looking a bit

grey. He had been underfed for months. But the blue of his young eyes had an intolerant green in them, like the green of ice.

'You must have been stuck in the bottom,' said Ronnie.

'God knows,' said Hugh.

They rowed out a long way. They were frightened now to use the second line. Hugh could not see any gulls about to signify herring. Some of the Golspie men had said you could smell herring. An awful fear was growing in him that this waste of sea would take everything and give nothing. When he had fallen and bumped the bottom boards, there had flashed through his mind the words: 'Between her two skins of tar she's rotten.' He knew this joke against them was going the rounds. The old Golspie man was supposed to have made fools of them.

Quietly Ian asked: 'Can you get a queer sort of smell, or am I imagining it?'

'I've got it for some time,' said Ronnie. 'I think I know what it is.'

'What?' asked Hugh.

'It's not herring anyway,' Ronnie answered, with slow sarcasm.

'What is is?' demanded Hugh shortly.

Ronnie looked at him, the smile on his sallow face pleasantly bitter. 'It's the smell of our burnt homes.'

It was a dank sooty smell, faint, evasive, but quite unmistakable. At the mouth of the strath itself, they would hardly get it, but here away from the usual land and animal smells, the air they breathed was very clean. The recent rains must have turned the old blackened homesteads into sodden heaps, and now the winds as they eddied down the glens and joined forces on the sea, brought the sodden smell in occasional whiffs.

None of them spoke. The skin on their faces had turned pallid and their eyes were round and restless. The shore by the mouth of the Ullie was hardly more than a dark line. The hills behind went inland in smooth clean curves. They knew these hills. Without an individual memory touching consciousness, a whole immemorial way of life went through them like a blade thrust.

Broken by their chief; man, woman, and child driven from the glens their forebears had held since the dawn of time. And to that bitter defeat – now this growing sense of defeat by the sea. They had sold good cattle to get this boat and gear. They had set out from the Ullie shore as the hope of the disinherited – to come upon this heaving immensity, barren, treacherous, and deep as death.

'We're drifting,' said Hugh. Then he noticed Torquil on his knees in the bow, his back turned to them, his head down.

'What's wrong with you, Torquil?'

'Nothing!' snapped Torquil.

'Feeling sick?' asked Ian gently.

His body gave a convulsive spasm. He retched, but there was nothing in his stomach. Ian caught him by the shoulder, looked down at his hands. 'What's this?'

'Shut up!' Torquil's face was grey-green but taut as a bow. He had whipped a single hook to the end of the broken line, and a foot or so above the hook had knotted the line about a slim stone. 'Give me the bait!'

His fingers shook as he handled the hook. Over the yellow pulpy limpet baits, his mouth opened and his chest caved in. But he baited the hook as Hugh had done and dropped it over the side.

They watched him, fascinated, until Ian noticed an increasing slant on the line, and put out an oar. Ronnie took the other. Experience was teaching them that they must 'hold up' a boat against the wind-drift. They pulled gently as if to make no noise, for they now had a strange premonition that something was going to happen.

As Torquil worked the line up and down, no one spoke. Torquil seemed to be listening to the line. Suddenly he began hauling the line in with such speed that his arms got meshed in its coils. The rowers forgot their oars. Hugh's mouth fell open a little.

When Torquil involuntarily stopped pulling, they craned over the boat and saw the grey back of a big fish. The sight unnerved them. 'Stand back!' screamed Torquil, and catching the line low down he heaved. The hook and line parted company as a great cod fell thrashing on the bottom boards. Instantly Hugh lunged at it as if it were a dangerous jungle beast and tried to throttle it. Finally he bashed its head against a seat. From the dead but still quivering fish, they lifted their eyes and looked at one another.

'Torquil, my hero!' said Hugh softly. He began laughing huskily. They all began to laugh. They swayed and hit one another great friendly thumps.

'Lord, we'll do it yet, boys!' said Ronnie.

They would do it! They would yet save the disinherited, by the sign beneath them! The great fat belly of the sign made them rock with laughter.

But Torquil had now discovered his hook was gone. When they found it inside the cod's mouth, they could hardly retrieve it for the weakness that mirth had put in their fingers.

But now Hugh was busy with the second line. When, after a fierce hauling, he produced a single little whiting, he could do no more than nod with helpless good humour.

They got going in earnest. The prospect of coming home as successful fishermen was very sweet. By the time the darkness was gathering, they had nearly a score of whiting and haddock as well as Torquil's cod.

'It's at the grey of the dawn, when the tide is on the turn, that they really feed.' said Hugh.

Their bait, however, was now getting scarce, for whiting are great robbers and so light on the nibble that one can hardly feel them. So they decided to shoot their net and hang on to it through the darkness. They had found the fishing ground and it would not greatly matter for a first outing whether they got herring or not. The net would act as an anchor and perhaps keep them on the ground. The wind was falling as had been foretold.

By the time the net was shot and they lay close together stretched out under the two rowing seats, an oatcake bannock divided between them, the night was calm and the sky full of stars. The boat rose and fell on the long gentle undulations of the sea. The mystery about and under them was now deeper than ever and they spoke in whispers. They spoke mostly of what they hoped to do for their people who had been so cruelly wronged. This kept their spirits up and sleep farther from them than the stars.

It was in the dark hour before morning that Hugh, lifting his head over the gunnel, saw the lights on the sea. In a moment the others were on their knees. They knew only one legend of the sea. It was about a ship sailing along with flame coming up from her hold and a Black Man playing a fiddle and dancing against the flame. They knew who the 'Black Man' was, though no one dared mention his name.

None of them spoke. Far in by the mouth of the Ullie small points of red fire could be seen where their own folk kept watch through the night. Their instinct was to haul the net very quietly and steal away towards that shore. But no one spoke.

'It's only a ship,' said Hugh.

'It's coming no nearer,' said Ronnie, who felt it coming nearer the more he stared.

'Great ships must have lights up at night,' said Torquil. They argued this, but Torquil was dogmatic, and they were beginning to have respect for him as a lad of good omen, a lucky lad.

'I believe you're right,' said Ian.

'Wouldn't it be great,' said Torquil, 'if the net was full of herring!' His incipient sickness, partly induced by excitement, was now gone. He felt a force in him fit to do astonishing things.

They began to be reassured. There was no flame and no Devil, anyway. On the contrary, the lights looked tall on the sea and calm as God's eyes.

When the sky paled and the first breath of the dawn flawed the smooth water, the lights of the ship went out, and they saw her, bare-masted, in towards Berriedale Head, a broad pale line running along her dark hull. As they looked, they saw her sails being shaken out, one after another, one above another, until she stood forth in all her high magnificence of billowing canvas.

The sight frightened them a little. Where such stateliness existed, there must be power, and with power – cruelty.

'I'll tell you what we'll do, boys,' whispered Hugh. 'We'll just lift the net and make for home. We've done well for one night.'

Ronnie and Ian agreed. Torquil was for having one more shot at the fishing; but even his protestations were half-hearted. There was a weak early-morning misery on their cold bodies. 'I think it must be the smell of the herring that's making me feel so empty,' said Hugh with a bleak smile.

But surprise had hardly begun to touch them yet. When they started to pull in their anchor line, they found the net was full of herring.

The new problems involved in hauling net and herring aboard made them forget all about the ship. Misery vanished in a sticky heat of excitement. They all shouted orders, for herring were falling back into the sea before their eyes. They nearly upset the boat twice. Voices rose tense and sometimes angry. The net seemed to be sinking with the weight of herring. They stood knee-deep in the living silver fish and the net was not yet half in. They began to be afraid of losing the net altogether. They pulled inch over inch, distributing their weight so as to keep the boat on a fair keel. Sometimes a voice broke into laughter out of sheer anxiety and the incredible nature of their luck. What was happening to them was beyond the maddest fancy of the long confidential talks they used to have before they had plunged into this wild venture.

'The ship is coming this way,' said Ronnie.

'Let her come!' said Hugh.

'There's a boat coming off from her,' said Ronnie.

'Let her come, too!' said Hugh. But they paused in their labours. Eight oars dipped and rose. 'Hurry up, for God's sake!' said Hugh.

But before the net was in, the ship's boat was alongside. There were twelve men in her. The four Kildonan lads had no English and could not understand what a very important-looking uniformed man was saying to them. He spoke as one having the powers of life and death.

Hugh turned from him dumbly and, with his companions,

set about the tail-end of the net so strongly that it tore away and sank under its weight of fish. When they turned back, they found that the ship's boat had them in tow.

At sight of the chain that had been slipped through their ring-bolt, mad anger flamed up in Hugh. The man who had spoken was watching him from the stern of the ship's boat. Two men sat beside him with muskets.

The tall ship put about and came into the wind close to them. Sails flapped. Men ran out on spars. A ladder and ropes came down the ship's side.

The four Sutherland lads took their stand in their own boat, knee-deep in herring, and the fight with the pressgang began.

It opened simply enough. 'Come on, you!' a man said to Hugh, and as Hugh did not come, he stepped in amongst the herring to take the Highland sheep by the ear.

'Don't you touch me!' cried Hugh in Gaelic.

'Oh, come on!' said the man, thrusting out his hand.

Hugh hit him under the jaw. The man stumbled backwards, straddled the low gunnel, and toppled into the sea.

There was a moment's intense hush. Then the whole towering ship broke into happy excitement.

In the end, his head laid open, Hugh was hauled aboard unconscious. Torquil followed him on the rope, hands tied and a bright gash over his left eye. Ian and Ronnie were helped up the ladder with the muzzles of the muskets.

The ship's crew, chortling over this bit of unexpected fun, tried to get a look at the native warriers and to pull the legs of those who were still spitting salt water.

'Them's the blokes wot've been turned out of their homes by sheep!' said one of the press-gang, as he rubbed his ear. 'Just shows you wot bloody yarns they spin us!'

When the fresh fish had been got aboard, the fishing boat was cast adrift.

The watch-fires on the slopes by the Ullie paled in the clear silver morning. Behind them the long suave lines of the hills caught a mist of rose. Slowly the bows of His Majesty's frigate fell away from the wind; the many sails bellied once more; and the stately ship set a southerly course.

# Snow in March

*Scots Magazine, 1938*

She went out to have a last look at her plants. The grass bank
in front of the old farmhouse had been rank with timothy,
dandelions, bishopweed, and one or two stunted unflowering
shrubs, before she had cleaned it up and turned it into
something like a rock garden. Her brother had got one or two
of the farm hands to help in the navvy work; and, for the rest,
it was a bit of a joke to him. That had been in the off-season,
before last harvest. At the first threshing of the harvest he had
been standing by the new machine, when the slim top cover,
not properly put on by the second ploughman, had been shot
by the whirling mechanism to the roof, whence it rebounded,
hit him with a sharp corner fair in the temple and killed him.

The blues were predominant: grape hyacinth, scillas, and
glory of the snow, with the aubretia coming along. It was
always a marvel to her how fragile these early flowers were.
The yellow crocus was a tuning fork out of some sunny
underworld. The snowdrops, delicate in their green veining,
chaste in their bowed heads, nun-like in their pallor, would
surely shrivel at a harsh breath. Marvellous to think that the
mature, lusty growths of summer would shrivel in weather
that gave to crocus and snowdrop a lovelier grace, a more
glowing colour.

Ah, and here at last some flakes of white – on the wild
cherry tree! Her heart gave a bound. She had lived through the
long winter for this. She had said to herself she would see one
round of the farm year before she sold the old place and went

back to her school in the city. And now, in the bright cold air, behold the cherry blossom!

As she gazed at the blown petals, two or three more petals came blowing past them. Snow petals. Snow! She looked into the depth of the air and saw the flurry of myriads of snow-flakes, not falling, but swirling darkly in the air, like swarming bees. Then they began to shoot past in front of her, all white; to settle on the flowers, her hands, everywhere. A ewe bleated beyond the garden wall in the home field; day-old lambs answered in their thin shivering trebles.

She woke sometime in the dark of the night and heard the young voices crying out in the field. They sounded forlorn and lost. The snow had been an inch deep before she had gone to bed. How much deeper now? The sheep were Leicesters and the grieve had told her they were soft because they were so well bred. Though actually an arable farm, it had always been famous for its sheep. The men folk had taken a pride in breeding them. This had been the tradition, and her brother had kept it up, making money even in the worst of the slump by buying sheep in small parcels from near and far and sending them south, for he knew all about sheep markets.

In the darkness the bleating of the lambs was very affecting. And there came one thin, persistent plaint that she knew instinctively to be the crying of a new-born lamb. She thought of the heavy ewes, square market-bred ewes, soft, having their lambs out there in the snow. She wished she could do some-thing for them.

She became restless and wide awake. *Waulkrife* was the Scots word. How deep went the native word, down through the muscles and round the bones to the roots, the last thin roots that went about the heart and gripped it, so that if you pulled them up you could hear the sound of everything tearing out – leaving an emptiness, a blank. A flurry of snow against the window, blind fingers against the glass, before the eddy of wind bore them away. Bore them away in a small, whining, anxious sound into space. Nothing conveyed the idea of space so well as the wind at night.

And all the time the lambs kept bleating, bleating, and the wind carried away their emergent bleating into the gulfs of space in a way the heart could hardly bear.

To ease this burden, her mind presented her with a clear picture. She was out in the field, going from ewe to ewe, gathering the lambs, carrying in her arms those that could hardly yet stand, and taking them all into the kitchen, where there was a good fire in the range and warmth and comfort.

Her whole being craved to do this, and suddenly in the thought of doing it was a profound mothering joy. Involuntarily her arms crossed and hugged her own breast.

That made her think, for she had developed the disease of thought, the analytical mental effort that affects instinctive action like a poison. For all that was troubling her was the mother instinct, or in her case presumably the mother complex, for the instinct had been denied, and as she was now forty she realised that it was probably permanently denied.

That's all it is, she told herself, and felt the roots of her virgin body thin and sinewy about a contracting heart. And recognising this in a bitter way, a hopeless agony, she had her own sorrow, and in a sudden spasm cried soundlessly except for a small, whining sound behind her nostrils.

Whereby she recognised, more certainly than ever, what was wrong with her, and for a time, in a release of irony, used all the psycho-analytic words that expressed her case. She had been German mistress in a Lowland academy until last June, when her mother had died, and, after the funeral, she had decided to stay on to keep house for her brother (her father being no more than a childhood memory). The decision had been the easier because of the headmaster, whom she had disliked for his thoughtless bullying. But also she had had an urge to get near the soil and the ways of the soil, the manner of life that had been her forefathers', not for any specific reason, but simply out of a vague longing, which she joyously refused to analyse because of its air of adventure. With her qualifications and experience, she could get a job again when she wanted one, for she had a reputation in educational circles.

She was quite an authority on German literature, particularly modern German literature, and kept in personal touch with the Continent. She could discuss the devious ways of Viennese psychiatry with some knowledge, even to the extent of quoting apt case-histories.

And here was the joyous adventure: listening to the ewes and the lambs, out in the snow, and being reminded of motherhood and defeat!

What about all her theories now, her precise knowledge, her apt case-histories?

This self-questioning was crude; she knew it was crude; yet the crudeness had an appalling reality, like the lambs with their red birthmarks in the driving snow, the mother licking them in the whirling snow, each lick making them stagger.

Or the cherry blossom.

The bleating would presently be too much for her. Emotion would rise up and up until it got hold of her head and drove her forth.

For her little intervals of ease, of half-mocking amusement at herself, were getting less frequent, less assured.

Quite suddenly, in a lull of feeling, there came upon her a deep compulsion to have it out with herself; as if she had dodged the real life issue until this moment, but now could no longer do so. It stared at her, and she stared back, her mind stripped, her eyes with pain in them, wanting to glance to left and right, but held by the lonely naked figure of herself on the lonely earth.

In the town, in her work, in her travelling and reading and social contacts, her societies and committees, she had seen the truth all right; nay, she had learned the truth, for was not that what education or book-study was for? For learning. A fine, wise word, against a background of good manners. And a lovely word, too!

But she could not slip away on the vague emotion induced by a word. The ruthless mind behind her mind was not going to be taken in any more by an easy trick. It had been tricked long enough by words, by labels, by analysis, and above all by the continuous movement, the brisk contacts, the fun and importance of social life amongst the more or less intelligent. In these days the intelligentsia suppressed nothing – in talk, at least. Compared with former generations, they were liberated, freed from inhibitions.

A harsh sound came through her nostrils, an irony that heard all their talk as the chattering of monkeys. For in this talk they were hiding themselves, without knowing it. Hiding themselves more than ever, because they were imagining they were evacuating their emotions. As indeed in a sense they were! They were continuously dosing their emotions and instincts with medicinal words. Trying to abolish their secrecy, to wash them clean. And feeling a sort of hectic ease as the process appeared to work.

But you could not go on purging and washing the instincts and emotions and expect them to fructify. You had to bury your seeds and put a roller over the earth above them, and keep them down, out of sight, certainly out of sight of the rookery, if you wanted them to fructify and sprout and become the stuff and the staff of life!

Her intuitions became so extraordinarily acute that a whole argument was apprehended in a flash of pain, as all motherhood was contained in the anxious cry of the ewe, and birth in the pitiful bleating of the lamb.

And when she grew exhausted, the crying from outside continued to play on her mind like an irritant, exquisite, clamant, ever more urgent. The night assumed fantastic proportions, extended into vast moorlands, endless wildernesses, immense gulfs of space, wherein the snow whirled like infinite manifestations of the physicist's dead atoms. And always spiring into this, the lamb's cry; the frail, blind, brittle cry, the first cry, the beginning of life – at last clutching at her heart, washed clean of words.

Driven out of bed, she pulled the curtain aside. The snow shower had passed and the sloping lands lay spectral white under the stars. Something in the whiteness of utter purity, of chill, virgin austerity, of light, touched her to a half-frightened wonder.

She dressed quickly, and in the kitchen went quietly lest she wake the servant girl. Into her long gumboots, her heavy mackintosh, tightening the belt about her waist; then to the back door, which she opened carefully.

The snow was surprisingly full of light and this suited her secret purpose, for she could not have taken a lantern. She did not want to be seen. She wanted to slip through the dark of night, unobserved, from ewe to ewe, intimately, from lamb to lamb, seeing that all was well. The universal mother, the mother of night! The sublimation of motherhood!

The labels were a secret joke now, and she smiled to herself as she got over the fence, for the air had a biting nip. Yet not a bleak coldness. Life was in it, left over from recent good days, something of promise, of spring. Glory of the snow.

She was suddenly full of a bounding, secret invigoration, and when some of the beasts, with lifted faces white against their grey fleeces, looked at her coming and, instead of showing fear, cried to her, taking even a step or two towards her, she was moved to cry back to them softly: 'It's all right. I'm coming. Don't worry.'

As the bleating increased all across the field, she got into quite a stir of excitement, and kept speaking softly all the time, so that she might be at home with them and her mind not distracted or invaded.

As her dark figure went about the field, it began to snow, and soon she was wrapped about in the whirling flakes and completely blinded, so that she could not see a yard in front of her, and when the wind got into her open mouth it roared there and choked her. She stood quite still, her back to the wind, leaning against it. The complete irrationality of her position, its futility, was a joy. For it was not quite so irrational as all that, she cunningly told herself. Not quite! And she got blown along a bit and kicked into a ewe giving birth to a lamb.

On her knees she could half see what was happening. Something deep in her sensitive nature had told her long ago that such a business would make her squeamish, would urge her away from it, as from something too intimate, as all blood is intimate, and coloured by primordial fear or terror.

But now, to her amazement, she was not repelled at all, she was not even overcome by her own inexperience and helplessness. On the contrary, she was charged by a confidence full of the utmost tenderness and optimism. She spoke to the beast, sheltered her, encouraged her, caressed her with a tender hand, wisely, helping her, used terms of endearment in a practical voice. And, as though some of her vitality and encouragement were indeed of practical assistance, the ewe had a short and easy delivery.

'You're feeling it a bit cold now!' she said to the lamb; and then turned on the ewe: 'Don't get excited, you old fool!' She would shelter them until the shower passed. She looked half over her shoulder, but the laugh died in her throat, for coming upon her was a smother of yellow light, swinging, growing – at hand. She rose up.

At that the light stopped and there was a harsh exclamation. Her slender-coated figure, rising snow-white like a ghost above the crying of a newly-born lamb, in the whirling ebb of the shower, might have startled a less sensitive mind than a shepherd's. In a moment she knew what was happening and cried to him by name. 'It's all right, Tom.' She kept crying to him to give him time. Took a step or two towards him. 'It was foolish of me to have come out without a light.'

'I wondered what you were,' he said at last with a touch of grim humour, wondering actually why she had come out at all. Could she not trust him to do his job? Was that it?

And she could hardly explain! But his natural suspicion did not down her good spirits, though it made her a bit shy. So she talked in an easy, friendly way, evolving the half-lie that she had thought a ewe was in difficulties, the cries had wakened her, and she had come out to see if she could help.

She soon had him thawed completely. There was a dourness in him, but once you got him out of that he could be friendly, even show a certain charm. He was probably about thirty-five and came from the north of Sutherland. Amongst her folk of the Moray country she had already noticed him. For she knew his type quite well; had even suffered a little herself in an innocent affair of student days with a youth from the glens. Whether this type became a student or a shepherd was largely a matter of economic luck. But the type had a natural friendliness at such a moment as this, because the atmosphere, the difficulties, the world around, suited the old nomadic spirit. His quiet voice conveyed a complete confidence, a sheltering reassurance. The environment revealed him.

'There's a ewe over there I'm worried about,' he said presently, when he had got to the top corner of the field. She was now all glowing with warmth. The shower gone, what had been half-frightening in the still, white landscape was no longer so.

'We have been lucky,' he said. 'But we cannot expect it to hold. They are pretty soft.'

So that when they came to the ewe that he had been worried about, she was prepared for death. He did everything he could with a strange concentration. When he spoke to the woman, he was speaking to himself. She sensed his deep, instinctive skill. The lamb was born, but the ewe died under his hands. On his knees, widespread in the snow, he looked at the humped body, his hands hanging.

He got up and said quietly: 'I'll take the lamb to the bothy. We may have a mother for it soon enough.'

'Come into the kitchen,' she said. 'I'll make you a cup of tea.'

The kitchen, with its hot water, was often of service in the ailments of beasts and regularly for the washing of milk pails and pans.

'Don't you bother, ma'm,' he said. 'I have the fire on and could get the milk for the lamb in no time.'

'Come,' she said calmly. 'I would like to give you a cup of tea.' And she moved on.

She did not want to lose him now, did not want to lose his company, did not want to lose sight of the lamb. And she did not even smile at herself. What she wanted she wanted.

He began tugging at the stiff latch of a cross-barred gate with one hand. 'Give me the lamb,' she said, and took it from

under his arm, holding it as he had held it. He opened the gate
and let her through.

As they came by the deep shadows of the house she paused
and looked back. 'Do you think it is going to be much?' she
asked.

'No,' he said. 'There is life still in the air.'

'The wireless forecasted snow-showers and outlook un-
changed.'

'Did it?' he said politely, cleaning his hands with snow.
'Come in.'

He scraped his boots clean. 'I'll make such a mess of your
floor.'

The bleating of the lamb sounded startlingly loud inside. He
struck a match and cupped it under his face. She saw the glow
of the light in his brown skin and the glitter of it in his dark,
attractive eyes. He needed a haircut. His eyebrows were
gathered together in concern. Then his face cleared and
opened as he tilted it up, and she said: 'Here's the lamp,' softly,
as if she might awaken the house.

He took matches out of his pocket and lit it while she stood
beside him. 'Now,' she whispered, 'if you go out to the shed
next the dairy you'll find some boxes there and straw.'

She stood on the middle of the floor listening to his footsteps and making soothing noises to the lamb. 'Hsh-sh!' she
crooned, and cupped her hand under its head, her fingertips at
its mouth. The fragile body butted, the little bones slithering
under the thin skin. The head waggled again. 'Hsh-sh!' And
she saw the discoloured skin and her own hands and wrists.
But, again, instead of repelling her, the streaks of blood gave
her a curious thick comfort. He came in with the box and put
it on the floor by the kitchen range. 'Now,' she said to the
lamb, and placed it in the straw.

'It's a feed he wants.'

'I know.' She nodded. 'I'll wash my hands and then put on
the fire.' She was no longer excited by the crying of the lamb.
The eager anxiety had passed into a calm of efficiency and
knowledge. Life was a healthy glow. She liked the way he took

the sticks Jean had drying over the oven and set about putting
the fire on. There were red embers still under the ashes. He put
a wisp of straw over the red embers, the dry sticks carefully on
top, and blew. Up came the flame and he built a few coals
around it. She poured some milk into a pan.

'You haven't a feeding-bottle?'

'No,' she answered slowly, trying desperately to conjure a
bottle.

'I'll be back in a minute with one,' he said, and went out at
once.

She smiled at that idiotic momentary dismay. As if she had
been about to lose something! And holding the pan over the
briskly-crackling sticks, she put a little finger into the milk,
moved it around, and then transferred the milk-dripping little
finger to the lamb's mouth.

She laughed softly to herself at the lamb's antics. And by the
time he had returned she had the kettle over the flame, with no
more water in it than would make tea for two, so that it would
boil quickly.

They still kept talking in undertones, and thus was spread
about them an amusing and warm air of conspiracy. Here was
natural life, and he was adept at all things concerning it. It
went back to beginnings in time far beyond rationalisings and
labels. The knowledge gave her a sense of freedom, lifted her
utterly beyond complexes and other strange modern diseases,
gave physical well-being a lovely ease.

She put a tea-cloth over the corner of the large white-
scrubbed table and set two cups on it and biscuits, and added
a friendly, bright air with knives and butter and plates. 'Leave
him now and wash your hands,' she said.

Artificial restraint, after the first few minutes in the field,
had passed quite away from him, and now in their friendly
work his manners were easy and good. One small trick he had
of looking sideways with a smile had recalled to her, almost
startlingly, her old student affair.

She was lifting the teapot to fill his cup when a noise arrested
her. The noise came nearer. She knew it was Jean, but could

not say a word, could not move the hand with the lifted teapot. They both stared at the door. It opened – and, her face half-petulant and flushed from sleep, there stood Jean, the servant girl. Her eyes widened as she gazed at Tom, and then right down her neck, as she turned her face away, went a deep blush. Dark, well-made, with a clear skin, she was inclined to moods occasionally, but was a capital worker. At this moment, in her twenty-fifth year, she looked extremely attractive.

'Come in, Jean,' said her mistress quietly. She glanced at Tom. He was looking at his plate.

The emotion between them, whether it had ever been declared or not, was so obvious to their mistress that her hand shook with the knowledge of it as at last she poured out Tom's tea.

'You're up very early,' she said to Jean.

'I heard the lamb and I wondered,' said Jean, her back to them, attending to the fire.

'Put some more water in the kettle, because there's hardly enough tea here for you.'

She began telling Jean about their experiences in the snow, disjointedly, while she drank her tea, so that the whole affair of their being thus together became normal and without strain, if still with an undercurrent of excitement, not in her own mind now, but self-consciously between these two.

'Well, I think I'll have an hour or two in bed. What's the time? Five. No need for you to hurry, Tom.'

She left them and went up to her room.

She was feeling very tired now, but when she had undressed and stretched between the cold sheets she experienced a pleasant sensation of ease, almost as if she had become disembodied. A crush of snow, softer than the lamb's mouth, smothered itself against the window. And all at once she thought of the ewe – that she had quite forgotten – with the head thrown out and back, the neck stretched to an invisible knife. The snow would be drifting about the body, covering it up.

She began to cry soundlessly, effortlessly.

# A Brief Note on the Short Stories

1. 'The Dead Seaman', first published in the *Scots Magazine* in July 1931, was modified and incorporated into *The Key of the Chest* (London: Faber & Faber, 1945). The brother Charlie becomes one of the principal characters in the novel and after many tribulations participates in a 'happy ending' through his reciprocated love for the minister's daughter Flora. The claustrophobic atmosphere and tragic process of the short story are thus subverted through its absorption into an episodic novel with several sub-plots and a romance dimension. Chs I–VI form an expanded but modified version of the story, while the repercussions of the finding of the dead seaman interact with the other motifs in the overall plot. The printed copy held by the NLS has been lightly emended by Gunn and this is the copy text reprinted here. Changes in the main remove superfluous adjectives and/or explanatory phrases, thus giving the text a greater economy and tension, while the rewriting of a passage at the end of section IV transforms a somewhat self-conscious account of the intimacy between the brothers into the communication of a deeply-felt emotion.

2. 'Birdsong at Evening'. The printed copy held in the NLS has been heavily emended in Gunn's handwriting. The first thirteen lines have been cut out, thus omitting the explanatory 'scene-setting' of the story, while several sections, some of page length, have been rewritten. Again many of these emendations remove explanatory phrases and superfluous adjectives and descriptive images, many of them of a 'purple' nature. As a result the story as a whole becomes more taut and one is more aware of its gently ironic tone, something which renders the slightly improbable ending more believable – or at least helps one to suspend disbelief.

3. 'Strath Ruins'. This early story anticipates the excitement of the many poaching episodes in Gunn's later novels while pointing

towards the more positive relationship between people and landowner envisaged in the optimistic *The Drinking Well* of 1946. The story itself, however, was not reused by Gunn in any of his later novels, despite the compatibility of its theme.

4. 'The Man Who Came Back'. The subtitle of this story is 'Study for a One-Act Play' and the narrative is carried as in a play through the dialogue between the principal characters Iain and Granny Cattanach, the silences between Iain and his father and the interchanges with his father's friends who visit the crofthouse. First published in the *Scots Magazine* as a story in 1928, it was developed into the play 'Back Home' and published in book form under that title (Glasgow: Wilson, 1932). The theme was clearly one which greatly preoccupied Gunn. It was explored in serialised and book form in *The Lost Glen* (Scots *Magazine* 1928 and Edinburgh: Porpoise Press, 1932) which has a tragic ending, and in *The Drinking Well* (London: Faber & Faber, 1946), this time with an optimistic outcome. It recurs, again negatively, in *The Serpent* of 1943, although the story-line and setting of this novel are quite different from those of the closely related works mentioned above. The theme questions the myth of the 'lad o' pairts' and the deeply ingrained belief that 'doing well' inevitably means leaving the Highlands, while it simultaneously explores the Highlander's emotional attachment to his land and the negative aspects of life in small, isolated communities. The paradoxical responses of love of land yet unwillingness to believe in its future are also recurring themes in Gunn's periodical articles of the thirties and forties.

5. 'The Storm'. This story of 1935 was to have two reincarnations. It appeared in an expanded and rewritten form as 'Ride the Gale' in the American *Saturday Evening Post* of 16 December 1950 and as an episode in the novel *The Well at the World's End* (London: Faber & Faber 1951). The novel episode follows the rewritten 'Ride the Gale' as opposed to 'The Storm'. Names are changed and the perspective is that of the storm-bound old sailor, his son and experienced crewman as opposed to the watchers on the shore as in the original story. An animosity between father and son is developed – something absent from the first version – while the love interest which is lightly sketched in in the early version and is clearly on the periphery of the action, is more fully developed in 'Ride the Gale' and the novel. The unity and economy of 'The Storm' in my view triumphs over the later, more elaborate version.

6. 'The Boat'. First published in 1937, this story was later incorporated into the opening chapter of *The Silver Darlings* (London:

Faber & Faber, 1941). Although names were changed and the story carefully revised and reshaped, the vitality of its communication of the innocence and optimism of the new fishers and the tragedy which overtakes them is preserved in the novel version, which in its overall pattern and import follows the story closely – something which may have come about as a result of their proximity in time.

7. 'Snow in March'. This 1938 story was modified and incorporated into Part Two, Section 3 of *The Shadow* (London: Faber & Faber, 1948), where it serves as a reminiscence by Aunt Phemie about her younger life. The brother of the short story becomes Phemie's husband in the novel, while her childless situation is the result of a miscarriage, not a consequence of her decision to choose spinsterhood and an intellectual life as in the story. The NLS printed copy has a very few emendations in Gunn's handwriting. As with the alterations in other stories, these are mostly to remove superfluous words and phrases or to replace an image with a more simple and specific one, as in the change of 'tropic clime' on the first page to 'sunny underworld'. The principal change is the excision of the final sentence: 'The tears ceased and she fell into a deep sleep', which seems to wrap the happenings up in a comforting ending and thus deny the pain and the awareness of irretrievably lost opportunities which the story so powerfully communicates. The new ending: 'She began to cry soundlessly, effortlessly' is more open and appropriate, allowing as it does the sense of pain and loss to stand. As with previous stories containing emendations by Gunn on the printed copy, the altered text is the one reproduced here.

# Sources

'The Dunbeath Coast' appeared in *Caithness Your Home*, ed. Herbert Sinclair (London: Sinclair, 1930), p.3, reprinted in *Whispering Winds* (Edinburgh: Thomson, 1975), pp.6-7; 'At the Peats' in *Chambers's Journal* XIII, 12 May 1923, pp.369-71; 'White Fishing on the Caithness Coast' in *Chambers's Journal* XIV, 4 October 1924, pp.708-10; 'John o' Groat's in *Chambers's Journal* XV, 10 January 1925, pp. 81-3; 'Highland Games' in *Scots Magazine* XV No.5, September 1931, pp.412-16; 'The Ferry of the Dead' in *Scots Magazine* XXVIII No.l, October 1937, pp.13-20; '"Gentlemen – The Tourist!": The New Highland Toast' in *Scots Magazine* XXVI No.6, March 1937, pp.410-15; 'My Bit of Britain' in *The Field*, 178, No.4623, 2 August 1941, pp.136-37; 'High Summer by a Mountain Lochan' in *Scotland's Magazine* 56 No.6, June 1960, pp. 10-11; 'Nationalism and Internationalism' in *Scots Magazine* XV No. 3, June 1931, pp. 185-88, reprinted in *Landscape and Light*, ed. A. McCleery (Aberdeen University Press, 1987), pp. 177-80; 'Preserving the Scottish Tongue: A Legacy and How to Use It' in *Scots Magazine* XXIV No.2, November 1935, pp.110-11; 'The Myth of the Canny Scot', undated typescript in National Library of Scotland deposit 209, Box 9, No.102, pp.l-9; 'Memories of the Month: A Balance Sheet' (under pseudonym of Dane McNeil) in *Scots Magazine* XXXIV No.4, January 1941, pp.258-62; 'For Christopher's Cap', undated typescript in NLS deposit 209, Box 8, No.45, pp.1-2; 'Is There a Living Scottish Tradition in Writing Today?' in NLS deposit 209, Box 9, No. 83, pp. 1-4, broadcast in 'Scottish Life and Letters', BBC Scottish Home Service, 15 January 1959; 'The Dead Seaman' in *Scots Magazine* XV No.4, July 1931, pp.265-89, emended copy text in NLS deposit 209, Box 4, No.12; 'Birdsong at Evening' in *Cornhill Magazine* LXI, September 1926, pp.298-314, emended copy text in NLS deposit 209, Box 4, No.4; 'Strath Ruins' in *Chambers's Journal* XVII, 3 September 1927, pp.625-30; 'The Man Who Came Back' in *Scots Magazine* VIII

No.6, March 1928, pp.419-29; 'The Storm' in *Scots Magazine* XXII No.5, February 1935, pp.349-57; 'The Boat' in *Scots Magazine* XXVIII No.3, December 1937, pp.186-94; 'Snow in March' in *Scots Magazine* XXIX No.3, June 1938, pp.191-99, emended copy text in NLS deposit 209, Box 4, No.41.